ROSTREVOR
History, Place, and People
～ PART 1 ～

Patrick Murphy

Rostrevor: History, Place, and People
by Professor Patrick Murphy

Copyright ©2023 Professor Patrick Murphy

ALL RIGHTS RESERVED

ISBN 978-1-916620-17-9

Including the right of reproduction in whole
or in part in any form.

This edition printed and bound in the Republic of Ireland by

lettertec

Lettertec Publishing
Springhill House,
Carrigtwohill
Co. Cork
Republic of Ireland
www.selfpublishbooks.ie

This book is dedicated to
Anna, Catherine and Matthew
so that not only will they know
about their home area of Rostrevor,
they will also understand it.

Acknowledgements

I wish to express my thanks to my family for their help and support in the production of this book. Particular thanks to Patrick for his academic insight and expertise across many areas, including morphological analysis, solar interpretation and cartography.

Introduction

This book is the first part of an attempt to chart the history of Rostrevor, County Down, and its surrounding area. It is neither final nor infallible and should be regarded as a work in progress to which others may wish to offer additional knowledge and analysis. It is based on available evidence and it will no doubt be revised and updated as new information emerges. This first part covers the period from the earliest times to about the middle of the 16th Century.

Many accounts of Rostrevor's history have been mythical, manufactured or romanticised. Challenging popular myths and long-held beliefs with a fact-based analysis will hardly be popular. However, we owe it to future generations to lay the foundations for a more comprehensive and reliable account of our past.

The overall aim is to focus largely on the parish of Kilbroney, but since history tends not to confine itself to geographical boundaries this account extends, where appropriate, to adjoining areas.

All history begins with geology. Rostrevor's history is no different and all around us we can see this area's origins in the landscape - if we know where to look. If we do not understand our geology, we cannot analyse our landscape and without that analysis we cannot gain the necessary insight into our places and their original names, the patterns of human habitation and the evolution of our society and economy.

However, there is an inherent challenge in presenting local history: who exactly might want to read it and how can its style and content be shaped to satisfy that readership? Should it be written for the general reader, or should it be tailored more towards an academic style work, with sources properly referenced?

This publication tries to cater for three possible categories of reader. For those with a specialist interest in local history, it offers an academic-style list of sources to support or authenticate a piece of information or an opinion. The references at the end of each chapter are specifically designed in a user-friendly format so that anyone can use them and the number of references has been kept to a minimum.

The second group includes those who do not want to read the book from cover to cover, but who may wish to use it as a reference tool - something to be referred to when curiosity raises its head about a particular place or an event in history. In that context it may be used to settle an argument, although it may start the odd one too.

Then there are those who want what might be called a coffee table book. To cater for them, each chapter is prefaced with a short summary of its content, which will either draw the readers in to seek more detail or propel them rapidly to the next chapter's summary. The photographs may help to supplement, or even replace, the narrative.

Some of the history may be dry and dull and other parts may be more interesting. But that's the point about history - you can't make it up. All we can do is to describe it in a manner which explains it impartially and as accurately as possible, within the limits of currently available information.

Those who do not know Rostrevor see it solely in terms of scenery. Those who know and understand it, recognise that it is much more than tourist-style photographs. Rostrevor is a way of life, a philosophy and a series of values and non-sectarian attitudes which place the common good above individual self-interest. That unique, collective personality of Rostrevor outshines those claiming to be individual personalities.

This Rostrevor ethos can best be retained and explained by using the everyday language of Rostrevor people. For that reason the text uses locally used place-names which are clarified in a section at the end of the book.

It contains townland names and their origins, which still shape much of the local language and explain aspects of the local geography. It also contains the names of places which the people here have used for much of the 19th and 20th Centuries.

This publication only scratches the surface of our local history, but if it inspires others to pursue the subject in greater depth, with accuracy, impartiality and rigour, it will not have been in vain.

Some of our history is local in origin. Some has come to us as part of our national history and some is derived from world events.

Whatever its origins, all of that history has been local in impact and while this book is divided into sections for the purposes of reading, it is a seamless story which meanders through historical time and geographical space to bring us where we are today.

Wherever that meandering leads to in the future, the true character of Rostrevor will endure and this book is a first step in offering an opportunity to appreciate its unique history, its special place and the spirit of its people.

Patrick Murphy
Kilbroney
October 2023

x

Contents

CHAPTER 1

Rostrevor's mountains, hills and coast, viewed from across Carlingford Lough.

Landscape and Scenery

The Kilbroney Valley: created by earth movements, sculpted by ice and later cultivated by humans.

Chapter 1 Summary

How it all began…

This chapter attempts to explain how Rostrevor's mountains, hills, rivers and coastline were developed and shaped. The photograph at the beginning of this chapter shows the countryside from the drumlins on the left, through the older uplands in the centre, to the more recent granite hills above Rostrevor on the right.

This landscape is built on a foundation which is nearly 500 million years old. It consists of a rock called greywacke, which can be seen throughout the parish, from the face of Leacan Beag on the Kilbroney Road to the sharp rocks, generally dipping Southeast, on the shore at the Monument.

It is generally dark grey in colour and can be made up of a range of materials from sand, gravel and mud, which were laid down by underwater currents on the sea bed.

These rocks were later pushed upwards in a succession of movements by molten magma, which did not reach the earth's surface. The magma cooled to form various types of granite, which appear on the surface today because the overlying rocks have been removed by erosion. The granite in the Rostrevor area tends to be pink or brown in colour, unlike the grey granite found in other parts of the Mournes. Greywacke and granite have been used for hundreds of years to build our houses, factories, churches and bridges.

The formation of the Mournes was accompanied by rifts in the earth's surface which caused some parts of the landscape to slip down relative to the adjoining land. Much of the Kilbroney Valley, for example, was formed by a fault, the face of which can be seen today in the wooded slopes on your right as you travel up the Newtown Road.

In more recent times, ice advanced over Rostrevor's landscape and shaped the existing topography by scouring the mountains, carving out existing valleys and forming drumlins (small, elongated hills) to the North and West of the village. It also brought loose rocks from other areas, including Cloughmore and deposited them here.

When the ice melted, its weight was lifted from the land which then rose, causing the sea level to fall. This has resulted in a steep embankment along much of our shoreline, marking the difference between the old sea level (at the top) and the present sea level (at the bottom).

The most obvious places to see that embankment today is the hill in Mary Street. The former sea level was at the Square. This difference in the two sea levels can be also seen along the Warrenpoint Road and the Shore Road, particularly at the Promenade.

This uplift of the land also caused what are known as river terraces along the steep sides of some of our rivers. They appear as shelves along the valley sides and they are best seen in the Drumreagh valley.

The old sea bed underlies much of the land between the village and the Monument Corner, including St Colman's Gardens and St Jude's Gardens, which in the 1950s were prone to flooding.

Today some of the original landscape has been masked by modern housing and other developments. However, the bulk of Rostrevor's natural beauty remains untouched and the landscape's formation and development can still be easily recognised and understood. It was into that landscape that the first settlers arrived here and how they adapted to it informs the content of Chapter 2.

480 million year-old rocks on the slopes of Leacan Mór

Chapter 1 Rostrevor's Foundations

Geology

The rocks on which Rostrevor stands had their origin at the bottom of a tropical ocean, about 480 million years ago.[1] They date from what is known as the Ordovician-Silurian period, when colliding continents pushed up marine sediment to form mountains. One continent was Laurentia, which at that time was about 15 to 20 degrees South of the equator. It contained most of what is now the North of the British Isles, including Rostrevor.

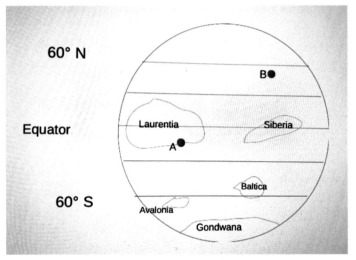

Fig 1.1 Rostrevor's approximate location about 480 million years ago was at A. It is now approximately at B on the new continent of Europe.

The rest of the modern British Isles was located on Avalonia. Between them was the Iapetus Ocean. As continents came together, the sediment on the bed of the ocean was pushed upwards to form mountains, which now range from the Appalachians in the Eastern USA, through Novia Scotia, Greenland, Iceland and Ireland to Scotland.

The main rock type from this period is greywacke, which is characterised by its hardness and dark colour. It can be made up of a range of materials from sand, gravel and mud, which were laid down by underwater currents on the sea bed. It does not normally contain fossils, even though the first fish and first land plants were emerging on earth at that time. The lines showing the layers of sediment are still clearly visible in many locations around Rostrevor. They dip towards the Southeast at an angle of about 50° and they underlie much of South and East County Down.

Fig 1.2 Greywacke strata on Rostrevor shore between the slipway and the Woodhouse. (In all photographs, the white ruler represents one foot or 30 cms.).

The remains of that system can be seen as rock outcrops in various places around Rostrevor, including the rocks on which Cloughmore rests; the jagged rocks on the shore at the Monument Corner and Killowen Point; on the shore beyond the Quay on the road to Kilkeel; at the Salmon Leap in the Fairy Glen and on the rock faces at the front and rear of Leacan Beag[2] on the Kilbroney Road. There are numerous small-scale examples of the folding in the rocks which created the mountain ranges mentioned above.

Fig 1.3 Greywacke folding on Leacan Beag as indicated by the red line.

Fig 1.4 Small scale folding of greywacke on Rostrevor shore near the Woodhouse. The red line shows the pattern of folding.

About 65 million years ago, during the Tertiary Period, further continental movement led to the development of a rift in the earth's crust, resulting in the beginnings of the Atlantic Ocean, when Ireland was about the latitude of where Southern France is now.[3] The stretching of the earth's crust caused large volumes of molten magma to erupt on to the earth's surface in South Armagh and North Louth. (That same volcanic activity continues today in Iceland.) The first activity occurred across Carlingford Lough from Rostrevor, in what is known as the Carlingford Igneous Complex. There, Slieve Foy consists of several layers of the igneous rock gabbro, which gives the mountain its distinctive colour. This was followed by other igneous activity in South Down, but here the molten material did not reach the earth's crust, although it was later exposed when the overlying rocks were eroded.

Instead, it intruded into the Silurian greywacke, at a high level in the earth's crust in a series of igneous intrusions to form the Mourne Mountains. Each intrusion caused large sections of the existing rocks to subside. There were five major intrusions of molten material. They cooled to form five different varieties of granite, which have since been exposed by erosion. Two of the intrusions (known as G4 and G5) occurred in the Western Mournes near Rostrevor. Today, remnants of the "roof" of original material can still be found on Finlieve, to the South of where the Yellow Water River rises and on the Southeastern slopes of Slievemeel, to the South of Kilbroney Red Bog.

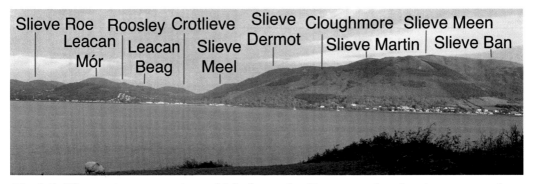

Fig 1.5 The main mountains which form the Rostrevor landscape as seen from across Carlingford Lough.

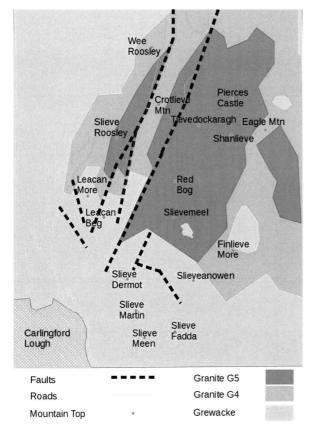

Fig 1.6 Simplified geological map of Rostrevor area.

Granite emits radon gas, which is colorless, odourless and radioactive. Although not all of Rostrevor is underlain by granite, the local council's building regulations require all new buildings to have a special membrane to stop the gas seeping into buildings.

So, the Rostrevor area contains the complex interface between the Silurian greywacke and Tertiary granite. This interface can be clearly seen today in most of the stone walls locally. A fine example can be found in St Bronagh's Church in Kilbroney cemetery. (Fig 1.7) However, neither greywacke nor local granite is suitable for intricate carving and the nearest example of fine stone work can be found at the castle in Greencastle, where quoins and other dressed stones are made from local limestone.[4]

Fig 1.7 Granite and greywacke intermingled in the wall of what is commonly referred to as St Bronagh's Church in Kilbroney Old Cemetery. The granite rocks are marked with a 'G'. They are pink or brown in colour and tend to be rounded, because of the way they weather. The greywacke is more straight-edged.

Although the colour of the granites in the Rostrevor area can vary, depending on the details of their chemical composition, they tend to range from pink to brown, unlike the predominantly grey granites in the rest of the Mournes. A good example of Western Mournes granite can be seen on the right-hand retaining wall as you walk down to the Slope on Rostrevor shore. When the wall was raised in height about 2005, the original capstones were removed and then replaced, but the extra height was gained by using other forms of granite as the photograph indicates. (Fig 1.8)

Fig 1.8 Local granite and granite imported from other parts of the Mournes at the Slope.

Since Western Mournes pink/brown granite is particularly difficult to shape or carve, it tends not to be used for any form of intricate stone work. (Although there is one claim that it may have been used to make stone axe-heads, it is too vague to pursue.[5]) For example, it was used to build much of the bridge on the Shore Road in 1881, but for the face of the arch, the builders used granite from other parts of the Mournes. (Figs 1.9 and 1.10.)

Fig 1.9 Bridge over the Kilbroney River at the Shore Road.

Fig 1.10. Detail of bridge showing grey Mourne granite used for decorative work on the arch, while the pink/brown Western Mournes granite is used for building the bridge.

The closer it was to the igneous activity, the more the greywacke was changed by the heat of the molten material. Although normally a clearly stratified rock, some greywacke was effectively melted and hardened in a manner which removed its clear lines of sediment, making it remarkably difficult to break. Local farmers referred to boulders of this type as "a blue", pointing out that if you tried to break it with a sledge-hammer, "it will just go into a ball".[6]

Igneous activity also forced a number of intrusions into the greywacke, which can be seen at various locations around Rostrevor. Most of the intrusions are in the form of dykes, which are solidified sheets of magma cutting across the older rock beds. Because the igneous rock in the dykes is more resistant to erosion than the greywacke, the dykes tend to form ridges in the landscape.

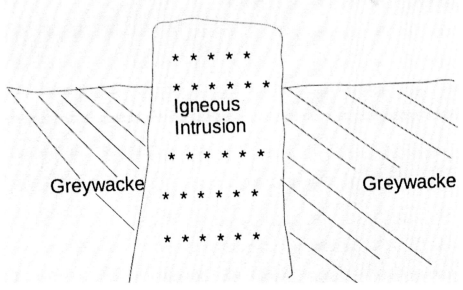

Fig 1.11 Simplified diagram of dyke showing the igneous rock extending above the surrounding country rock because of its greater resistance to erosion.

There are a number of these dykes in the Rostrevor area, the best examples of which can be seen on the Eastern face of Leacan Mór. They were first identified in an 1881 geological survey of Ireland as "felstone porphyry among Silurian Rocks, Leckanmore Hill, above Rostrevor".[7]

They can be seen in Fig 1.12 as four ridges on the face of Leacan Mór and one each on Leacan Beag and Knockbarragh Mountain, better known as Slieve Roe. The area to the right of Leacan Beag is underlain by the main igneous mass which extends beyond the skyline and includes the wooded area to the right of the photograph. The dykes are most obvious at sunset, particularly during the winter months (Fig 1.13)

The dykes in the accompanying photographs are part of a much wider distribution of igneous intrusions in the Rostrevor area, emanating from the igneous mass which formed the Mournes.

Fig 1.12 View from Cloughmore looking Northwest towards Knockbarragh (Slieve Roe), Leacan Mór and Leacan Beag, showing the ridges (marked in yellow) created by igneous rocks which are harder than the surrounding greywacke.

Fig 1.13 Shadows of the igneous intrusions on Leacan Mór created by the setting sun in January.

Fig 1.14 Vertical dyke near Cloughmore as indicated by the yellow lines. The 30 cm white ruler can be seen horizontally on the right of the dyke.

The heat from these intrusions metamorphosed (changed) the greywacke immediately beside it. This can be seen about 200 metres South of Cloughmore (Fig 1.14) where a dyke is clearly exposed intruding into the local greywacke. What appears to be the same igneous intrusion can be found on the shore near the Woodhouse on the road to Kilkeel, about half a mile past the Quay. A similar igneous intrusion has been quarried in the area behind what is now Campbell's garage. The rock in this quarry has been traditionally referred to as syenite.[8] This is generally believed to be the reason for the name Syenite Place where, it is assumed, the quarry workers were housed.[9] More recent tourist literature has suggested that the rock was not syenite, but diorite. The truth is that it was neither syenite nor diorite. It was most probably another igneous rock, known as gabbro.

Fig 1.15 Igneous intrusion on the shore below the Woodhouse. (The entrance to the Woodhouse can be seen as the white pillar at the top of the photograph.). This may be part of the same igneous intrusion which emerges over 200 metres up the hill beside Cloughmore.

The explanation[10] for the confusion probably lies in two factors: (a) geological terminology has changed over the years and (b) greater scientific understanding and analysis has allowed a more accurate classification of rocks. The term syenite was presumably a misunderstanding of the rock type, based on the presence of the mineral hornblende in the gabbro. "There has never been any true syenite in the Rostrevor area."[11] Although diorite was reported in the initial geological field survey, this was likely incorrectly named at the time[12] or the terminology has subsequently changed. "There has also never been any diorite in Rostrevor.[13]" The quarry is part of an igneous dyke which runs up past Cloughmore and on to the townlands known as The Point Park and Ballinran Upper.

Earth Movements

The igneous activity in the Rostrevor area produced a number of faults, which occur when stress causes a fracture in the rocks and one side of the fracture moves, vertically and/or horizontally, relative to the other. A generalised outline of the faults is shown in Fig. 1.6.

The steep slope running parallel to Newtown Road (on your right as you travel away from Rostrevor) represents a vertical fault. The farmland on the valley sides and bottom is where the land slipped down relative to the higher ground. It extends, almost in a straight line, from Newtown Villas to beyond Hen Mountain.

Fig 1.16 The fault running parallel to Newtown Road, illustrated by the steep slope of the Kilbroney Valley. It runs at right angles to the fault along the face of Slieve Foy, on the opposite side of Carlingford Lough.

Fig 1.17. Fault on Leacan Beag, on the side away from Kilbroney Road.

Almost parallel to it is another fault. It runs along the back of Leacan Beag, again almost straight, following the line of Kilbroney Road to the top of Reed Hall and beyond towards Hilltown.

Fig 1.18. The fault viewed from Leacan Mór. The land in the foreground has slipped down relative to the higher ground.

A shorter fault runs along the front of Leacan Beag. Finally, the face of Slieve Foy overlooking Carlingford Lough is also a fault line. (Fig.1.19) This makes the County Louth shoreline almost straight, as opposed to the more irregular County Down coastline.

Fig 1.19 The straight shoreline illustrates the Slieve Foy fault on the far side of Carlingford Lough.

Glaciation

Although geological processes formed Rostrevor's foundations, subsequent events shaped it into the landscape we recognise today. About 2.5 million years ago there began a series of climatic fluctuations between temperate and glacial. The glacial periods were caused by global cooling, which created vast accumulations of snow and ice in Northern latitudes and the resulting polar ice sheet expanded and contracted many times. At its most advanced, the ice covered all of Ireland, apart from what is now parts of Cork and Kerry, between 24,000 and 18,000 years ago. In this initial stage, the ice swept across from Scotland, covering most of Down and Armagh, shaping the Kilbroney and Drumreagh Valleys.

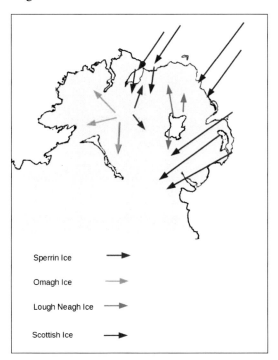

Sperrin Ice

Omagh Ice

Lough Neagh Ice

Scottish Ice

Fig 1.20 A generalised map of the initial glaciation phase, showing the movement of Scottish ice across South Down, including moving down the Kilbroney Valley.

Its impact can be seen on Leacan Beag, where the ice formed a steeper northerly slope and then a long extended downstream slope, which stretches through Levallyclanone down to Cherry Hill and Rostrevor village. It can best be seen from the Newtown side of Kilbroney Valley.

Fig 1.21 Leacan Beag from Newtown Road. The Scottish ice moved from right to left.

At a later stage, the ice swept Southeast from the Lough Neagh area and divided into two ice movements: one to the North and one to the South of the Mournes. The Southern movement is referred to as the Pontyzpass Ice Stream.[14] It carved

17

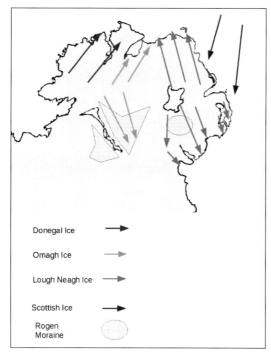

Donegal Ice ⟶

Omagh Ice ⟶

Lough Neagh Ice ⟶

Scottish Ice ⟶

Rogen
Moraine

Fig 1.22 Later stage of glaciation showing the ice moving down Carlingford Lough towards the Irish Sea.

out the lowland from Lough Neagh, following the line of the Belfast-Dublin Railway and the Newry Canal, down to Carlingford Lough and the Irish Sea. It deposited a series of sand and gravel landforms known as moraines, one of which stretches from Knockshee Mountain at Kilfeaghan in an eastwards arc down to Cranfield.[15] The area's history of excavating sand and gravel pits is based on this type of glacial deposition.

When the ice finally withdrew, it left a sculpted landscape and several erratics, which are glacially deposited rocks differing from the type of rock native to the area in which they rest. The obvious example is Cloughmore (*Cloch Mór*, big stone) a granite boulder resting on greywacke and there are numerous smaller erratics littered across the area, including on the top of Leacan Beag.

Tertiary Granite

Silurian Greywacke

Fig 1.23 Glacial erratic on Leacan Beag

18

Fig 1.24 Cloughmore (Irish: Cloch Mór meaning Big Stone), a granite glacial erratic sitting on Silurian greywacke with smaller erratics scattered around it.

As the ice advanced and retreated at various times, it created temporary lakes, one of which, according to geologist, J K Charlesworth, was in the hills above Rostrevor: "The ice imprisoned a small lake in the recess south-east of Rostrevor, its delicate terraces at a height of about 1000 feet O.D. on the western slopes of Slieve Martin (1595 ft), being readily discernible on a clear day from the Warrenpoint-Rostrevor main road. The morainic line of big granite boulders to which the well-known erratic of Cloughmore belongs was formed at a slightly lower level."[16]

Fig 1.25 The approximate locations of what Charlesworth (1966) referred to as "delicate terraces" on the side of Slieve Martin, represented by the lowering levels of what he claimed was a temporary glacial lake there formed as the melting ice was retreating.

The "terraces" to which he refers represent levels of the lake shore as it lowered. They are no longer visible from the main road, as they are now largely hidden by coniferous trees. The highest of them coincides roughly with the final part of the walkway from Cloughmore to Slieve Martin.

Sea Level Changes

The weight of the huge ice mass pushed the land down, causing the sea level to rise. When the ice later melted, the higher sea level meant that the Rostrevor shoreline was much further inland than it is today. The centre of Rostrevor, around the Square represents the old sea level as the ice began to melt and much of the village below that level would have been the sea bed, probably underlying a swampy estuary. This would have extended over much of the Warrenpoint Road area, including St Colman's Gardens, where the marine mud today reaches a depth of 9 metres in places. It also includes most of the land as far as the Monument, with small patches of slightly higher ground, possibly remaining above the sea. Nearer the village, the sea bed would also have included St Jude's Gardens, Greenpark Road around St Rita's, the Shore Road as far as the Promenade and the Kilbroney River as far up as the Bridge.

Fig 1.26 Mary Street: the seabed was previously at the bottom of the hill and the sea level was approximately where the cars are parked.

As the land slowly rose again, the sea level fell. The difference between the old and new sea levels can be seen today along most of the Rostrevor coastline, particularly along the Warrenpoint Road to just beyond Arno's Vale and along the Shore Road, particularly at the Promenade. The vertical difference between the two is marked by a steep slope, usually a few metres high. The new sea level is clearly at the bottom and the old one is at the top, which is usually referred to as a raised beach. The steep face of the raised beach has been made less steep by human modifications in some places, such as in the height difference between Greenpark Road and Greenpark Court and in the hills which form both Mary Street and Bridge Street.

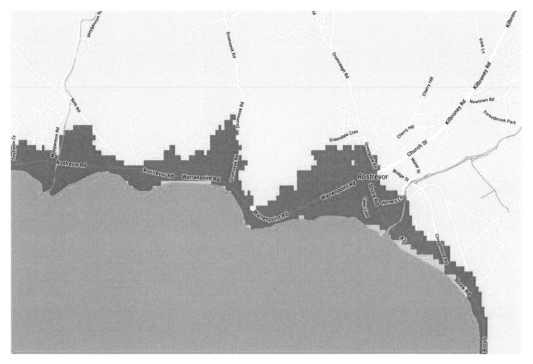

Fig 1.27 Areas of Rostrevor which were probably covered by the sea immediately following glacial melting. (Source: https://www.climatecentral.org/what-we-do/legal#content_licensing)

Fig 1.28 Raised beach along the Warrenpoint Road. As the ice melted, the sea bed would have been level with the top of the wall.

Fig 1.29 A more dramatic example of a raised beach can be seen at Kilkeel. where glacial deposits of sand and gravel form the steep face.

Fig 1.30 Flooding beside the Presbyterian Church in the 1950s. The houses in the photograph have since been demolished.

The sea would have extended upstream to near the bridge at the bottom of Bridge Street. The raised beach can be seen where the Meadow is much higher than Cloughmore Road. The old sea bed also includes many new houses on the Rostrevor side of the Kilbroney River along the Shore Road. It is disguised by the fact that when the Shore Road was built in the 1870s, it used large amounts of fill. This can be seen today at the point where Horner's Loanin meets the Shore Road. The field level is much lower than the road and regularly floods in winter. Even within living memory, the former sea bed regularly flooded, particularly at the junction of the Shore Road and Warrenpoint Road. (Fig 1.30)

The impact of the land rising after glaciation is also evident in local river valleys. There are four rivers in the Rostrevor area: the Drumreagh River, the Kilbroney River, which flows through the Fairy Glen; the Cassy Water, which marks the Eastern end of both Kilbroney parish and the Diocese of Dromore and Moygannon River, which marks the Western boundary of the parish. The level of the rivers at various post-glacial stages is shown in river terraces. These are terraces of land at various heights along the river banks showing the level of the river at different times as the land rose after the last glaciation. The best examples of river terraces can be found on the Drumreagh River in the Drumreagh/Knockbarragh valley.

Fig 1.31 Upper course of the Drumreagh (or Ghann) River: the river previously flowed at the level of the trees on the right-hand side. Its present course can be seen in the centre of the photograph.

Fig 1.32 The high ground on the right is where the river previously flowed before cutting down to its present level on the left.

Fig 1.33 A meander in the river's upper course has become incised because of the land rising and causing landslips on the slope.

Fig 1.34 Drumlin countryside to the West of Rostrevor.

The ice also created a number of drumlins[17] in the Rostrevor area. These are small, elongated hills made up of glacial depositions, which cover a significant part of lowland Ulster, including South Down. The best local examples can be found in the Drumsesk and Moygannon area to the West of Rostrevor

The landscape and scenery of Rostrevor have been formed through a complex series of geological movements, later shaped by other processes including ice and water. These processes have produced our current countryside, which was initially heavily wooded before the first humans arrived. When they came, they gradually modified the landscape in their own interests, clearing the woodland and ultimately farming the countryside. Our landscape would now be modified by human rather than natural influences. Nothing would be the same again.

Chapter Endnotes

1   Mitchell W I (2004) *The Geology of Northern Ireland* Geological Survey of Northern Ireland, pp 6-7.

2   According to Mooney's *Place Names of Rostrevor* (1950) p 26 *Leacan* means a place of flagstones. He has presumably based this on the word leac, which means a flagstone or the flat stone just outside the door of the house or forming the entrance into the house. *Leacán* tends to mean a small flagstone.

3   Baxter S (2008) *A Geological Field Guide to Cooley, Gullion, Mourne and Slieve Croob* Louth County Council, Heritage Council, Geological Survey of Ireland, p 13.

4   Ministry of Finance (1966) *An Archaeological Survey of County Down* HMSO p 131.

5   Jope E M, Morey J E, Sabine P A (1952) *Porcellanite Axes from Factories in North East Ireland: Tievebulliagh and Rathlin* Ulster Journal of Archaeology, 15, 1952, p 47.

6   Dick Murphy in conversation with me about 1980, when I was trying to break "a blue" with a sledge hammer.

7   Memoirs of the Geological Survey (1881) *Explanatory Memoir to Accompany Sheets 60, 61 and Part of 71 of the Maps of the Geological Survey of Ireland*, p 34 and p 43.

8   The name syenite comes from Syene (now Asswan) in Egypt, from where it was transported to build the heavy protective blocks above the king's chamber in the pyramid of Khufu.

9   Mourne Mountains Landscape Partnership (undated) *Rostrevor Village and Heritage Trail* claims that the quarry was managed by Joseph Weir from Liverpool who supplied "setts" (cobble stones) which were shipped to Liverpool from the Quay. The Belfast Gazette announced on September 23 1927 that the Rostrevor Syenite Quarry Company Ltd would be struck off the Company Register "unless cause is shown to the contrary". The company had obviously ceased operation.

10   E-mail from Dr Kirstin Lemon, Geological Survey of Northern Ireland 26.06.2020. I am indebted to her and to Dr Marie Cowen, Director of the Geological Survey for their help.

11   E-mail as above

12   Memoirs of the Geological Survey, p 42.

13   Email as above.

14   McCabe M, Dunlop P 2006 *The Last Glacial Termination in Northern Ireland*. Geological Survey of Northern Ireland and Ulster University p 1.

15   McCabe and Dunlop, p. 49.

16   Charlesworth J K *Some Observations on the Glaciation of North-East Ireland*. Proceedings of the Royal Irish Academy Vol 45 (1938-1940) p 287.

17   From the Irish word *droimnín*, meaning small hill or ridge.

CHAPTER 2

Kilfeaghan dolmen, a portal tombstone built in the Neolithic (New Stone Age) period about 4,000 to 5,000 years ago.

The First Settlers

The rocky Killowen shore where the first settlers were more likely to have landed than in the muddy Rostrevor bay just along the coast.

Chapter 2 Summary

The first people arrive…

Although we know that the first people arrived in Ireland about 9,000 years ago, there is no indication as to when the first human settlement began in Rostrevor. However, we can estimate their arrival from more general archaeological evidence.

The first arrivals on the island settled in the Bann Valley near Coleraine. They presumably came from nearby Scotland and it is likely that they eventually made their way down the East coast of Ireland by sea. This suggests that they explored Carlingford Lough and its shores. Evidence has survived of human settlement at Cornamucklagh, on the Louth side of Narrow Water. It dates from more than 6,000 years ago. Between then and about 5,000 years ago there was slash and burn activity to clear the forest along the Leitrim River (the stream on the right as you begin the descent from Reed Hall towards Hilltown.)

In clearing the heavily wooded land they used polished stone axe-heads, one of which has been found in Kilbroney. They began to domesticate animals and introduced a range of skills, including the ability to make clay pots.

Some of our understanding of this period comes from important pieces of evidence which relate not so much to the living as to the dead. Kilfeaghan dolmen (more accurately called a portal tomb) is built of granite and dates from about 4,500 years ago. It marks a burial site and it may have been used for various ceremonies.

Other surviving evidence from this period consists of a man-made pile of stones on the summits of various local mountains. These include Knockshee, Slieve Martin and, apparently Thunder's Hill, although little evidence of it remains.

The Stone Age was followed by the Bronze Age, which left little mark on the Rostrevor landscape. Possible surviving physical features include two (or maybe three) standing stones not far from the Kilbroney Road. When viewed from a nearby rath, they appear to relate to the movement of the sun on important dates in the ancient calendar. However, a definite conclusion on this issue will require further investigation.

The Iron Age lasted from about 500 BC to 400 AD. It is particularly noted for raths, which are circular earthen walls, forming enclosures and serving as settlements. There are numerous examples of them in the Rostrevor area, particularly in the townlands of Drumsesk and Moygannon. The old church in Kilbroney Cemetery is built in what was originally a rath.

Although most of the evidence from the Iron Age is recorded in the landscape, there is also surviving written evidence indicating that the Irish coast, including Carlingford Lough, was known about as far away as Rome. A map of Ireland drawn by Claudius Ptolemaeus (c100-170AD) better known as Ptolemy, was part of a wider map of Europe. It gives a description of this country at a time when there were few other references.

Rostrevor may not have existed as a formal settlement then, but its landscape was being recorded for the first time. This meant that it began to attract attention from overseas. The first result of that attention was the arrival of Christianity in Ireland and, as Chapter 3 will explain, Rostrevor played its part in that new era.

Kilbroney Valley in the November evening mist.

CHAPTER 2

Rostrevor's First Settlers

While the geology of the Rostrevor area can be analysed and described with scientific accuracy, the same cannot be said about the earliest human settlements here. Although there is some available local evidence, we have to rely largely on additional information from surrounding areas and from more general information about Ireland at that time. The prehistory can be usefully divided into three main ages: Stone, Bronze and Iron.

Stone Age

The first settlers arrived in Ireland about 9,000 years ago, initially in the Bann Valley near Coleraine. They were Mesolithic[1] (Middle Stone Age) hunters and gatherers, who most likely came by boat from Scotland. At this stage Ireland was an island, but Britain was still joined to Europe. This suggests that the first arrivals settled in coastal locations and river valleys opening on to the sea, presumably including Carlingford Lough. Evidence for their settlement includes a late Mesolithic site at Cornamucklagh, Co Louth, where the proposed Narrow Water Bridge is to be built.[2]

The settlers did not cultivate the land or keep animals and they appear to have exploited seasonal fruits, nuts and berries, as well as fishing and stalking large game. Because of the nature of their lifestyle, they left little evidence apart from stone tools. These include finds from Ballygarvan on the Ards Peninsula,[3] Annalong[4] and the Shimna River near Bryansford[5]. Since there is not an abundance of flint in South Down, some of the tools may have been brought here from elsewhere.

The physical evidence locally suggests that Killowen may have attracted the first settlers to the Rostrevor area, but since other relevant evidence may not have survived, we cannot be totally sure of this. However, since the first people here came by sea, the Killowen coast offered easier access to the land than Rostrevor bay, which has a huge tidal range. Certainly at low tide, the muddy Rostrevor coast is largely inaccessible from the sea and Mill Bay, on the other side of Killowen village, is even more tidal. Although the sea level was higher at that time, it is likely that Rostrevor bay was just a large swampy inlet.

Fig 2.1 Killowen Point where the first settlers are likely to have landed because of its accessibility even at low tide.

One of the earliest pieces of evidence for human activity in this area comes from just over the top of Reed Hall (on the road to Hilltown). It suggests that between 6,000 and 5,000 years ago, in the early Neolithic[6] (New Stone Age) period, there was slash and burn activity[7] to clear the forest along the Leitrim River (the stream on your right as you begin the descent from Reed Hall towards Hilltown). Because the upland forests were thinner, they were easier to clear. This indicates that people had begun to change their way of life, probably inspired by the arrival of new settlers. They began to farm the land and keep animals, introducing a range of skills, including the ability to make clay pots.

Fig 2.2 The Leitrim Valley looking downstream towards Sheep Hill

Fig 2.3 The result of slash and burn on a hillside in the Leitrim Valley 5,000 years later. The trees in the distance are conifers, planted in recent years.

The slash and burn activity in the lower reaches of the valley had little long-term impact on its fertility, but higher up, the destruction of trees led to soil erosion. This meant that in the long term, the vegetation cover was difficult to replace and the result has been the barren hillside we see today.

In April 2021 what appeared to be a polished axe head (Fig 2.4) was found in the demolished walls of what was originally an 18th Century house in Kilbroney, about 3 miles from the slash and burn site. It was identified by the National Museum of Ireland as probably dating from the Neolithic period and it appears to be the only

artefact of its type found in the Rostrevor area. It presumably typified the sort of tool used to clear the vegetation in the upper reaches of the Kilbroney Valley, including Leacan Mór, Slieve Roosley and Reed Hall, all of which are bare of trees to this day and support only heather.

Fig 2.4 Neolithic axe head.

One example of a Neolithic settlement near Rostrevor was at Ballinacraig, outside Newry, which dates from 4400 years ago to about 2000 years ago. Excavations there[8] in 2005 unearthed pottery shards, some of which date from the Early Neolithic period. The pottery fragments indicate the use of thin-walled, fine textured pots, with carefully smoothed surfaces, many of which are described as carinated. This means they tend to be rounded at the bottom, with straight sides near the top and an outward folded rim. Carinated bowl pottery has been found at many locations around Carlingford Lough including at Mourne Park and Ballyedmond. The Ballinacraig site also revealed coarse stone tools, mainly flint. Stakeholes, where upright wooden supports were placed, contained birch and hazel charcoal, which suggests some type of wattle screening or shelter for the settlement. It is reasonable to assume that similar settlements existed in the Rostrevor area.

Fig 2.5 Kilfeaghan dolmen (portal tomb) looking towards the sea.

There is also evidence from this period at Killowen, although it relates not so much to the living as to the dead. Kilfeaghan dolmen (more accurately called a portal tomb) is built of granite and dates from about 4,500 years ago. It is a single chamber megalithic tomb which marks a burial site and it may have been used for various ceremonies. Its traditional large capstone, elevated at an angle, measures about 2.5 metres long by 1.5 metres thick, weighing an estimated 35 tonnes. It is supported by two huge portal stones, which have partly sunk into the ground and the whole structure sits on a massive cairn which is about 15 metres long. It overlooks Carlingford Lough (Fig. 2.5) which indicates the close relationship between the first settlers and the sea. "Local inhabitants recall an unrecorded excavation in the chamber about 1912-1914 when bones and pottery were found."[9]

On the original pathway up to Cloughmore, just at the tree-line, there is another large structure which appears to have a capstone and supporting portals. However, it is largely buried, presumably due to landslip on the steep slope. It is not clear whether it is a natural feature of glacial deposition or a man-made structure, similar to Kilfeaghan dolmen. Only an archaeological excavation could determine its true origin.

Fig 2.6 Feature on the original path to Cloughmore

Another source of evidence is a court grave at Ballinran which was excavated prior to road widening in 1976.[10] Court cairns or court tombs are a form of Neolithic monument found across Ireland. Their form suggests that they were constructed for some kind of ritual or social events involving large gatherings of people. Initially referred to as a "Giant's Grave" in the first and second editions of the Ordnance Survey 6-inch maps (Sheet 54), Ballinran court grave was very large, aligned North-South with its outer end and forecourt facing the mountain. It was built on a 25-feet raised beach, in the third field on the right as you pass the entry to Killowen village on the road to Kilkeel.

It would have been much closer to high water mark at the time it was built than it is in more modern times. While it was still visible above the ground as late as 1874, much of it had been destroyed by then. The only finds in 1976 were cremated bones.

Ballinran was part of a dense grouping of court graves around Carlingford Lough, which suggests that the Lough was a main point of entry for those who built the court graves and who crossed the Irish Sea from Southwest Scotland. If they arrived in wooden-framed, skin covered vessels, they would have found Carlingford Lough a welcome shelter and they would have been glad of the additional protection provided by the Killowen Point spit.[11] (Fig.2.1)

In 1933 Estyn Evans excavated another piece of local archaeological evidence - the remains of a chambered cairn in Ballyedmond Park,[12] which had been largely destroyed for use in road building. It was constructed of local Silurian slabs and boulders and survived to a maximum height of about three feet. It measured about 56 feet by 40 feet and contained pottery remains similar to those found at Ballinacraig. Fragmentary bones representing at least seven individuals were found in small heaps in the gallery. The monument was close to the road which was marked on the first OS sheet (1834) where it is labelled "the new line". The older road is still in use today, taking a course further inland along the hillside. (The location of the cairn was 54°, 4′ 15″ North; 6°, 9′ 42″ West.)

Not all the evidence of human activity in the South Down area comes from within South Down. The world famous Newgrange passage tomb in the Boyne Valley was constructed about 5,200 years ago, before Stonehenge in England or the pyramids in Egypt. The cobbles on the entrance of the tomb came from the Carlingford Lough area: 41% are Newry granodiorite; 46% are Mourne granite (mainly G2, from the Eastern Mournes) and the rest are gabbro from the Slieve Foy area.[13] It would appear reasonable to assume that people in the Carlingford Lough area were involved in sourcing the supply of these decorative cobbles.

The only other surviving evidence from the Neolithic age consists of several cairns in the area. (A cairn is a man-made pile of stones. They may serve as monuments, burial sites or ceremonial grounds.) Hilltop cairns can be found on the summits of Knockshee, Slieve Martin and possibly Thunder's Hill along the perimeter of Big Dan's Wood, at the Levallyclanone side. They are also found along the Slieve Foy complex from where both the Mournes and the plains of Meath are clearly visible. As the Neolithic period drew to a close, megalithic monuments tended to be replaced by larger monuments of timber and earth, such as the Giant's Ring near Belfast.

Bronze Age

The dawn of the Bronze Age about 4,500 years ago, saw the gradual introduction of metal into the everyday existence of people here. It lasted for about 2,000 years. Around 4,400 to 4,200 years ago people in the Rostrevor area were extracting metals from the upper reaches of the Leitrim River, just over the top of Reed Hall, and the Carcullion River, which joins the Leitrim River further down the slope. Evidence from river sediment and metal analyses suggests the charcoal discovered may have been connected to the recovery of tin and gold.

It has been suggested[14] that gold from the Western Mournes was a possible source for some, although not all, of the Early Bronze Age ornaments. The Tellus project (Geological Survey of Northern Ireland) indicates that in sieved stream sediment, the incidence of tin across Northern Ireland is less than 5 parts per million (ppm). In the mountainous area of the Mournes it is almost always above 30 ppm and often rises to 40 ppm. There is no known evidence of prehistoric human settlement in the immediate area of the Leitrim River, so some of those involved may have come over Reed Hall from the Rostrevor side of the hill.

Generally, however, the Bronze Age left little trace on the South Down countryside. It has been observed that, "The relatively dense area of Neolithic settlement suggested by the court tombs of the Mourne-Carlingford uplands tends to shift to the east Belfast-Comber region during the early Bronze Age"[15] During this period existing tool types such as stone axes and flint knives were replaced with new forms made from copper and bronze (copper with about 12% tin). In 1938 a Bronze Age axe was found in a potato field at Ballymaginaghy near Castlewellan[16], but relatively few artefacts from this period have been found near Rostrevor. During the Bronze Age house types became circular rather than rectangular.

However, archeological evidence from the Bronze Age is difficult to find. Wooden structures have long faded, but there are three pieces of evidence from the late Bronze Age through to the late Iron Age which tell us something about Rostrevor during that period: (a) a map from the Roman Empire, (b) raths and (c) standing stones.

Iron Age

The Iron Age in County Down has been traditionally viewed as lasting from about 2500 years ago (when the Celts first arrived in Ireland about 500BC, replacing the hunter-gatherers who preceded them) to about 1600 years ago (400AD). While a Celtic language was spoken in Ireland from the beginning of the Iron Age, there is little material evidence for a Celtic "invasion". The Celts presumably arrived as part of a trading network and gradually assimilated into the local population. Theirs was a culture and not an empire, spreading from central Europe into these islands.

The transition to the widespread use of iron, in preference to bronze, appears to have happened slowly over a long period and it was not until the 3rd Century BC that a distinctive Iron Age society, clearly recognisable in archaeological records, emerged. The Iron Age is often divided into two phases: an earlier phase in which the North-east of Ireland adopted art styles and some metal workings from Europe and a later stage after the first century AD when Ireland was in contact with Roman Britain.

One of the few written references to the Irish Iron Age comes from a map drawn by Claudius Ptolemaeus (c100-170AD) better known as Ptolemy, who was born in Egypt, then part of the Roman Empire. His map of Ireland (c.140 AD), which was part of a wider map of Europe, gives a description of this country at a time when there are few other references. The actual map has not survived, but the co-ordinates he gives for various geographical locations allows us to reconstruct it.

Among the sixteen tribes he identified were the *Darini* whose name may be connected to *Dáire*. Dundrum in County Down is known as *Dun Drama Dáirine*.

To the South of them were the *Woluntioi*, who occupied an area stretching from *Emain Macha* (Armagh) to the *Buvinda* (Boyne). Among the rivers listed in his description are the Bann, which rises just North of Rostrevor and the *Winderios*, which refers to either Dundrum Bay or, more likely because of the size of the river flowing into it, Carlingford Lough. So Rostrevor's shoreline was first mapped (very roughly) about 2,000 years ago by the Romans.

Fig 2.7 Ptolemy's Map of Ireland.

40

Although the Rostrevor shoreline appears to have been known about by the Romans, they saw Ireland as largely uninviting, labelling it *Hibernia*, meaning "land of winter". They never came to Ireland, apart from occasional visits to what they saw as its hostile shore.

Raths

A rath (also called a ring fort) is usually a circular area surrounded by an inner bank of earth and an outer trench. The material dug from the trench was commonly used to build the bank. It had one or two openings in the bank for access. Where there were two openings, they tended to be opposite each other. The circular surround was often as much to keep animals in, as to offer defence against human and animal aggressors on the outside. The inner flat area of a rath is often referred to as a *lios*, meaning an enclosed area. In rocky or mountainous areas where it would have been difficult to form the rath embankment from soil, stones were used instead, often with no ditch. This feature was usually referred to as a *caiseal*.

Fig. 2.9 shows the distribution of raths in the Rostrevor area, most of them to the North and Northwest of the village. Although previously regarded as representing a very basic form of society, new research[17] in 2020 revealed that 30 miles from Rostrevor at Navan Fort in Armagh there was a vast Iron Age temple complex and ceremonial provincial centre. The massive earthworks were some six hectares in area, with the external bank measuring 13 metres wide and up to 3 metres high. It contained what were previously thought to be domestic dwellings, but the size and scale of buildings on the site now indicate a highly developed social order extending into the Christian era. The raths in the Rostrevor area were presumably open to influence from Armagh. This suggests that there existed a more advanced society in this area than we may have hitherto understood, particularly in view of the large number of raths here.

Fig 2.8 Generalised drawing of a rath

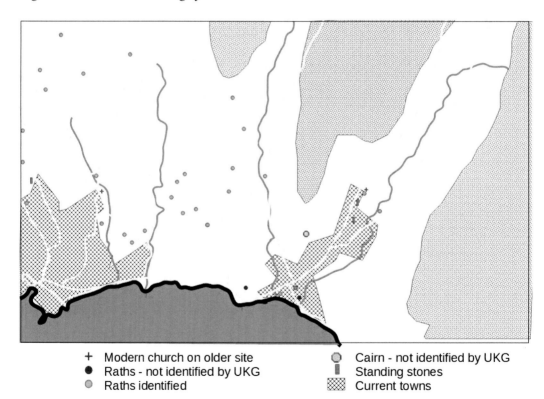

+	Modern church on older site	⊙	Cairn - not identified by UKG
●	Raths - not identified by UKG	▮	Standing stones
⊙	Raths identified	▨	Current towns

Fig 2.9 Distribution of raths in the Rostrevor area (UKG means UK Government agencies)

Fig 2.10 Six raths in close proximity in the drumlin country of Drumsesk.

Fig 2.11 Typical example of a rath in Drumsesk, looking towards Leacan Mór (left), Big Dan's Wood, also known as Ballymoney Wood (centre) and Slieve Martin (right).

This pattern of a circular settlement survived into medieval times and it is often difficult to date the origins of a rath since it may have been used over several hundred years, either in its original form, or as a result of one or more modifications. The wider Rostrevor area contains the physical remains and general outline of about

30 raths (Fig 2.9), suggesting continuous permanent settlement in the area for over 2,600 years. As well as the physical evidence on the landscape, additional insight comes from old OS maps and aerial photographs. The greatest concentration of raths in the Rostrevor area lies in the drumlin country to the West of Rostrevor, mainly in Drumsesk and Moygannon. Aerial photography shows that there was a number of raths in the Kilbroney Valley, but only two have survived intact, one on each side of the Kilbroney River. They may be of particular significance as illustrated later.

Sometimes raths occur in adjoining pairs as in Fig 2.12. Between the Moygannon Road and Levellyreagh Road on the eastern side of the Moygannon River are two raths about 150 yards apart. They are on a Southern-facing slope about 360 feet above sea level, overlooking Carlingford Lough, which is about three quarters of a mile to the South. In 1966 the upper one had a stone wall about four feet thick with an earthen ramp against the inside. It was about 150 feet across. The lower rath was about 110 feet across and of similar structure.[18]

Fig 2.12 Two raths to the East of Moygannon River (marked by the line of trees running across the photograph, left to right in the background) between Moygannon Road (just beyond the river) and Drumsesk Road (out of picture to the right).

One of the best surviving examples of a rath is on the Rath Road (also known by locals as Turret Hill), on the Warrenpoint side of the Moygannon River. It is generally known as Rathturret. (Fig. 2.13). While the "rath" part of its name is easy to understand, the "turret" is less so.[19] It is set about 150 feet above sea level on the slope at the Southeast end of a Northwest to Southeast ridge.[20] It is enclosed by three banks with ditches between them. "Approaching the entrance to the interior on the south-east is a causeway across the outer ditch, but there is no corresponding break in the middle or outer banks. There is no causeway across the outer ditch and a bridge must have been used."[21] Although it is difficult to get an overview of its structure because of the dense vegetation growth, the pattern of embankments and ditches still survives. It had a clear view down Carlingford Lough towards the Irish Sea.

Fig 2.13 Rathturret (top centre in the clump of trees), while the outline of an adjoining rath can be seen in the next field (bottom centre).

Fig 2.14 The inner embankment of Moygannon Rath with modern steps cut into it for access to the inner enclosure.

Fig 2.15 The inner enclosure is still clearly visible, although heavily overgrown.

Not all raths have survived, of course. One has disappeared in living memory along the Drumreagh Road, for example. Described in 1966 as "largely overgrown"[22], it was about 100 feet across on the edge of a scarp beside the Drumreagh River. "It has a bank 9-10 feet wide, with stone revetments traceable in places on both inner and outer faces. Immediately outside the bank on the North, and following its course, is a hollow in which runs a rough disused road."[23] The rath's disappearance was probably accelerated by Kilkeel Rural District Council's decision in the 1950s to use the river escarpment for what was then known as a dump, now generally called landfill. Other raths have been removed from the landscape through the historical expansion of arable agriculture, as happened with a rath along the Kilbroney Road. It can only be detected from the air by ground patterns during a particularly dry period. (Fig 2.16).

Fig 2.16 Outline of disappeared rath alongside Kilbroney Road.

While all of the above examples of raths are reasonably straightforward to interpret, there is one particular example which will require detailed excavation to determine its historical origins and evolution. In the area immediately behind the Monument, there are earthworks which, on initial examination, appear to be the remains of a significant rath. Its elevated position commands a strategic view of Carlingford Lough and it offers a clear line of sight to the locations of two other possible raths at the Crag and at Arno's Vale on the Rostrevor-Warrenpoint Road.

Fig 2.17 What looks like a rath in a figure of 8 (or even two adjoining raths) behind the Monument. Figure of 8 raths were commonplace at royal sites such as Navan Fort and Tara.

Fig 2.18 What appears to be a circular landform on the Warrenpoint side of the Monument.

What appears to be a standard circular rath pattern can be seen on the Warrenpoint side of the Monument, but the adjoining earth works suggest that if this was a rath, the site has been heavily modified at a later date. The possibility of later modification is shown in Fig 2.19, which illustrates that the cultivated field meets an irregular boundary, which does not quite conform to the traditional rath pattern.

Fig 2.19 The cultivated field meeting an irregular site boundary which is not in keeping with the traditional rath footprint.

Of equal significance is the fact that the site has not been identified as a rath (or indeed an earthworks of any importance) on any OS maps. However, it can be argued that the site would have been ideal for a rath with its unimpeded view down Carlingford Lough towards the Irish Sea. It was from there that any sea-borne threat would inevitably come. At the same time, it should be recognised that this site would also be ideal for defence at a later point in history and even for a display of authority or grandeur in subsequent centuries. A preliminary examination of the site offers a possible explanation for how it developed and that theory is explored in Chapter 4.

Fig 2.20 The site offers an uninterrupted view of the Lough towards the Irish Sea.

Since many raths were occupied and modified over centuries, it is usually difficult to distinguish between the various periods of occupation and the structures which existed within them. Raths were used as sites for domestic and religious settlements at later dates throughout history up to about 1100 AD. Some may have been used continuously for up to 1500 years. A fine example of the adaptation of a rath for monastic settlement can be seen in Kilbroney cemetery, one of two raths in the Kilbroney Valley.

Fig 2.21 The outline of the rath in Kilbroney Old Cemetery is clearly visible, as indicated by the white line highlighting the embankment.

Fig 2.22 The likely full extent of the rath.

In Ireland it is thought many of the Christian holy sites were originally symbolic landmarks for local communities since the Bronze and Iron Ages. These sites ranged from royal locations, burial cairns, raths, standing stones and wooden complexes to more sacred trees, groves and wells.[24] It would appear reasonable to suggest the Kilbroney church site held such significance and that a decision was made to build a church on the site and co-opt it to Christianity. Pope Gregory endorsed the approach to Christainise pagan settlements in AD601, and academics suggest many significant pagan sites were re-dedicated to Christian saints to disguise their pagan origin.[25]

Standing Stones

The Kilbroney Valley raths may be related to two or possibly three nearby standing stones. The classic standing stone surviving from the Bronze Age/early Iron Age in Ireland is a rough-hewn or unshaped pillar, known as a gallon (from the Irish *gallán*, meaning a standing stone) generally oval or oblong in cross-section and up to 3 m or more in height. They can be as small as one metre. Standing stones are generally aligned Northeast-Southwest.[26] "Their isolated positioning in the countryside, generally without associated diagnostic features, makes it difficult to provide a coherent archaeological explanation for the timing or context of their erection"[27]

However, the Kilbroney standing stones are perhaps unusual in that, if there are three, they form a perfectly straight line, running North-Northeast to South-Southwest. One is in a modern housing development in Pine Valley off the Kilbroney Road. The second is in the field beside the municipal cemetery (Fig. 2.23) and the third (if indeed it is a third) is in Kilbroney old cemetery (Fig. 2.24). Of course, there may have been more and these are the only survivors. The stone in Kilbroney old cemetery may have been a headstone, but it is greywacke and there are no other greywacke headstones in the cemetery. Indeed the oldest headstones are all granite. However, the stone is not marked as a standing stone on the earliest Ordnance Survey maps.

Their positioning and alignment may just be coincidence, or they may have some significance. Standing stones may have served as boundary markers, ritual or ceremonial sites, burial sites or astrological alignment. If these stones were boundary markers, we have no idea of exactly what type of boundary they may have been marking. Today they run more or less parallel to the Kilbroney Road, but since we do not know if there was a track or a path there about 4,000 years ago, we have no way of relating the stones to some form of route-way. Equally we do not know why there were only two or three standing stones. Were there more which, like so many raths, were removed and used for other purposes, such as building material? Or are these stones of particular significance?

It should be noted that Beaghmore standing stones in Tyrone have pillars of a similar size to those in Kilbroney, but with smaller stones (about the size of a football) surrounding them in circles. Such formations would be easily destroyed as the land was cleared and cultivated.

Fig 2.23 Standing stone in field beside cemetery.

Fig 2.24 Possible standing stone in the old cemetery.

One source of reliable evidence on the standing stones' function can be obtained from modern day observation on the ground. Theoretical models, such as suncalc, show the movement of the sun during the day at given locations, but when applied to the Kilbroney valley, they appear to rule out the role of the Kilbroney stones as astrological or astronomical markers. However, most models using sunrise and sunset positions apply only to a flat landscape. The Kilbroney Valley is far from flat.

So, any interpretation of the relationship between the two raths (in Newtown and Kilbroney) and the standing stones must rely on direct human observation of the sun's movement today. This may give us some indication of the function of the stones themselves, the design and location of the two rath sites and the potential importance of one of the sites, leading to its subsequent Christian takeover. Was the church built in the Kilbroney rath rather than the Newtown rath because it was also a burial site, as occurred in other parts of Ulster?[28]

What, if any, is the relationship between the raths and the standing stones? Is it linked to some solar pattern? The Kilbroney rath site allows an excellent view of the sunrise throughout the year. The Newtown site provides similar views of sunsets. For sunrises, the mountain silhouettes such as Slieve Meel and Slieve Dermot are marked with physical characteristics which can be used to accurately track sunrises across the year. These can be used to determine seasons and festivals without the difficult work of building astronomically aligned stone circles. The only omission from this annual cycle is the sunrise on the shortest day, but when standing in the Kilbroney rath on that date, the Newtown rath appears to mark the point of the sunrise.

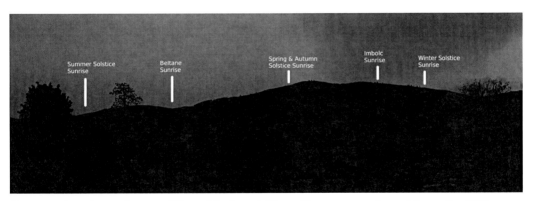

Fig 2.25 Sunrise points on Slieve Meel and Slieve Dermot as viewed from the Kilbroney rath.

In view of the darkness on the face of Slieve Dermot for about two hours before the sun appears over the mountain top, it might raise a question about the name of the mountain. Since there appears to be no evidence to link it to a Dermot, saint or otherwise, could it be that the name comes from *Sliabh diamhracht* (mountain of darkness, mysteriousness, bewitchment?) When the run rises to the right of Dermot, it is Halloween and later winter. When the sun rises to the left, it is the growing seasons. Of course, it may just be Darby's Mountain.

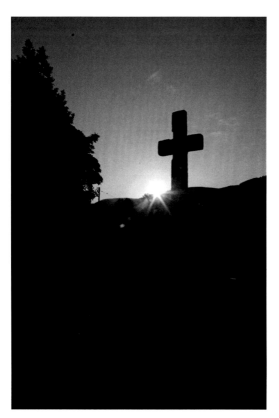

Fig 2.26 Sunrise at the summer solstice as seen from the rath in Kilbroney cemetery beside the old cross.

Significance of Raths and Standing Stones

From the Newtown rath, the sunsets are not as easily followed, as there are no obvious landform features. The sunset appears to align with peaks on Slieve Foy at the Celtic New Year, known as Imbolc and at Halloween, known as Samhain. Today these dates refer to February 1 and October 31. However, since the solar cycle is slightly variable each year, Imbolc could have fallen as late as February 6 and Samhain could have been up to a week later.[29] To disassociate the festivals from their solar origins, the Christian calendar later opted for fixed dates for these festivals and renamed them as St Bridget's Day and All Saints' Day.[30]

It is not possible to see the point of sunset from the Kilbroney Rath on December 21 because of the high trees which now separate the cemetery from the new municipal cemetery. However, by standing on the other side of the trees in the municipal cemetery, the sun can be seen setting in a dip in the Slieve Foy complex across Carlingford Lough. (Fig 2.27). It can also be seen from a higher vantage point (Fig 2.28) above the old church.

Fig 2.27 Sunset from the municipal cemetery

Fig 2.28 The same sunset from above the old church.

Fig 2.29 The standing stone in the field beside the cemetery is in line with the point of sunset when viewed from the Newtown rath. The yellow line indicates the actual line of sight and the orange line shows where the sun would set on a flat landscape. The base map is taken from Google maps.

During spring and summer the sun sets over Thunders Hill/Drumreagh/Levallyclanone, which have fewer clearly marked characteristics, resulting in a need to use stones to mark significant dates. This is most easily demonstrated at sunset on the May festival of Bealtaine (May 1, also known as Beltane) but it is variable by up to four days. Fig 2.29 shows the sunset on that date which aligns the Newtown rath with the standing stone in the field beside the cemetery. There are two large boulders at the far end of the rath which also align with the setting sun, but whether these are of historical origin or a more modern coincidence would require further investigation.

Fig. 2.30 Sunset at Bealtaine illustrating the line of sight between the Newtown rath (foreground) and the standing stone in Kilbroney (obscured by the sun's rays).

Fig 2.31 The rath in Newtown (circled on the left) and the standing stone in the field beside the cemetery (circled on the right). At sunset on the festival of Bealtaine (May 1, but variable by up to four days) the standing stone is aligned with the point of sunset when viewed from the rath.

Although the relationship between the rath and the standing stone appears to be clear cut, there is additional information which may, or may not, be relevant. The Bandy Bridge stream which possibly flowed past the rath and later the monastic settlement (See Chapter 3) may have followed the low ground in this field, as indicated by the white line. (Fig.2.32). Certainly this land is still prone to flooding in periods of heavy rain.

To one side of the probable stream course, where the modern electricity pole stands, is an elevated area of higher ground. Initially it might appear as a modern construct to facilitate the erection of the pole. However Fig 2.33 shows a detailed photograph of the pole from above. It indicates the possible outline of a roughly rectangular building on the site and the green area immediately close to the pole shows that those erecting it broke through the higher ground to get a foundation. The high ground and the possible building were there long before the pole.

We have no idea of the age of the probable building. It could be relatively modern or it could have some historical significance. We just do not know, but it appears that much of Rostrevor's pre-history still lies hidden beneath the ground. It will probably remain there because the sites referred to here are on private property and should not be interfered with in any way. If there are ever any further investigations, they should be left to the proper authorities.

Fig 2.32. The raised area where the modern electricity pole stands (in the centre) alongside the probably path of Bandy Bridge stream (in white) with the rath (left) and the standing stone (right).

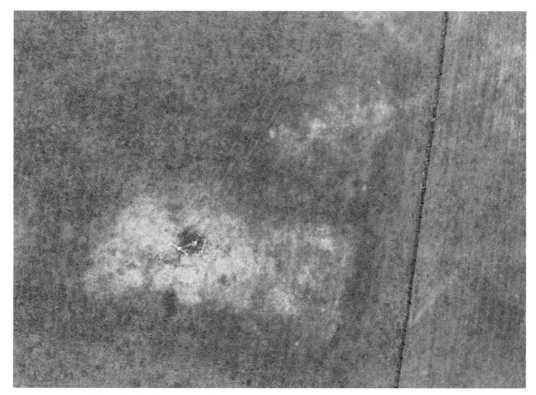

Fig 2.33. A detailed photograph of the electricity pole location. It shows a green circular area immediately close to the pole, suggesting that those constructing it broke through the higher ground for a foundation. A roughly rectangular building appears to have been on that site at some point in history, but we have no idea when.

The big question about the standing stones is why there were only two (or maybe three) of them. There may have been more, but it is possible that they could have been used as building material, particularly in the development of a monastic site around the old church. If there were other standing stones, they may have marked sunset at summer solstice and other points during the year. In the absence of more information, it is not possible to draw firm conclusions.

As well as raths and standing stones there are other references to physical features from the Iron Age. There is reference to a cairn at Thunders Hill in the townland of Levallyclanone, described as being "held in veneration by the inhabitants"[31] Although the area is forested today, it should be relatively easy to identify such a feature, but no trace of it appears to exist. It may have been in the same location as the setting sun at the spring solstice. If it was such an important feature in the 1834-36 OS memoirs, it is surprising that it was not recorded on the 1832 OS map. There is more work to be done on Rostrevor's pre-history.

The Iron Age lasted until about 400 AD. It is estimated that St Patrick arrived in Ireland in 432 AD, so the end of the Iron Age coincided roughly with the introduction of Christianity into Ireland. The old Celtic traditions of aligning man-made land marks with those of nature and the solar system was about to be replaced by a new set of beliefs. Many of the new customs and rituals would use the same sacred Celtic sites and dates as a framework for new religious practices. The Celtic and the Christian were about to be fused and, having played a key role in the old, Rostrevor was now about to perform an important part in the new. A new era was dawning for Ireland and Rostrevor would be an important part of it.

Chapter Endnotes

1   The Mesolithic period in Ireland lasted from about 10,000 years ago to about 6,000 years ago.
2   Walsh F (2015) Archaeological Excavations at Cornamucklagh, Omeath, County Louth, *Journal of the County Louth Archaeological and Historical Society*, Vol 28 No 3 pp 297-308.
3   Welsh H (2017) Survey Artefact Collection, Balygarvan, County Down, *Ulster Archaeological Society*. Report No 36.
4   www.bagenalscastle.com
5   McComb A (2005) Random Finds of Flint Objects in the Area of the Shimna River, near Bryansford, County Down. *Ulster Journal of Archaeology*, Vol 64, pp 172-3.
6   The Neolithic period marked the beginning of farming in Ireland.
7   Warner R B and Moles N R (2015) Radio-carbon dated charcoal from fluvial sediments in the Mourne Mountains, Northern Ireland: Neolithic forest clearance and tin and gold recovery in the Early Bronze Age. *The Journal of Irish Archaeology*, Vol 24, pp 97-114.
8   Sneddon D (2005) Prehistoric activity at Ballynacraig, Newry, County Down. *Ulster Journal of Archaeology*, Vol 64, pp 1-11.
9   Ministry of Finance NI (1966) *An Archaeological Survey of County Down* HMSO, p 80.
10   Collins A E P (1976) A Court Grave at Ballinran, County Down. *Ulster Journal of Archaeology*, Vol 39, pp 8-12.
11   A spit is an extended stretch of beach material which projects out into the sea, usually in a curve, and is connected to the land at one end.
12   Evans E E (1936) A Chambered Cairn in Ballyedmond Park, County Down. *Ulster Journal of Archaeology*, Vol 1, pp 49-58.
13   Meighan I, Simpson D and Hartwell B (2002) Newgrange: Sourcing of its Granitic Cobbles. *Ulster Journal of Archaeology* Vol 16, No 1 pp 32-35.
14   Warner and Moles
15   Mallory J P and Hartwell B N (1997) Down in Prehistory Chapter 1 in *Down, History and Society* (Proudfoot L (ed) Geography Publications p 23.
16   Evans E E (1944) A Bronze Axe from Co Down. *Ulster Journal of Archaeology* Vol 7, pp 98-99.
17   O'Driscoll J, Gleeson P, Noble G 2020 Re-imagining Navan Fort: New Light On The Evolution Of A Major Ceremonial Centre in Northern Europe. *Oxford Journal of Archaeology*, Vol 39, Issue 3, pp247-273.
18   Ministry of Finance p 181.
19   Nail Comer (2023), a highly reliable source for translating Irish place-names, wonders if it is based on tuar meaning, "a cattle fallow field" and that the "-et" at the end could be the remnants of the word *fada* meaning "long". So, the full title would be "Rath of the long, fallow, cattle field." *The Gaelic Heritage of Southeast Ulster*, Facebook, June 2023.
20   Ministry of Finance p 155.
21   Ministry of Finance p155.
22   Ministry of Finance p 172.
23   Ministry of Finance p 172.
24   See: Harney L (2017) Christianising pagan worlds in conversion-era Ireland: archaeological evidence for the origins of Irish ecclesiastical sites. *Proceedings of the Royal Irish Academy: Archaeology, Culture, History, Literature* Vol. 117C 2017, pp. 103-130;
Clay J.H. (2017) From conversation to consolidation in eighth-century Hessia. Making Christian landscapes in Altantic Europe: conversion and consolidation in the early Middle Ages pp 386-402. Cork University Press;
Lucas A T (1963) The sacred trees of Ireland. *Journal of the Cork historical and archaeological society*. 68, pp 16-54.
25   See: Blair J (1996) Churches in the early English landscape: social and cultural. *Council for British Archaeological Research* Report 104.
26   O'Sullivan M, Downey L (2020) Lone Standing Stones, *Archaeology Ireland* Vol 34, No 1, (Spring 2020) pp 26-29.
27   O'Sullivan M, Downey L p 27.
28   Lynn C J (1988) Excavation at 46-48 Scotch Street, Armagh, 1979-80. *Ulster Journal of Archaeology*, Third Series, Vol 51 pp 69-84.
29   https://earthsky.org/astronomy-essentials/halloween-derived-from-ancient-celtic-cross-quarter-day.
30   The Christian Calendar still uses variable dates for Easter, based on the cycle of the moon.
31   Day A, McWilliams P (eds) *Ordnance Survey Memoirs of Ireland, Parishes of County Down* 1834 - 6 South Down. Institute of Irish Studies, Queen's University Belfast p 29.

CHAPTER 3

The high cross, church and bell associated with St Bronagh.

The Rise of Christianity

A new dawn: sunrise at the winter solstice over the high cross.

Chapter 3 Summary

The Arrival of Christianity…

Christianity arrived in Ireland with St Patrick in 432 AD and local tradition has it that it soon made its way to Rostrevor. St Bronagh, after whom the parish and the townland are named (Kilbroney from the Irish *Cill Brónaigh* meaning Church of Bronagh) reputedly died in 512, having founded a monastery/convent in or near what is now the old cemetery in Kilbroney.

Despite the widespread tradition of St Bronagh in the Rostrevor area, we effectively know nothing about her. This is not to suggest that she did not exist, it is just that there is no reliable basis for any record of her life, as any written account dates from several centuries after her death.

The main source of information about Bronagh (original Irish spelling *Brónach*, meaning 'sorrowful') comes from various biographies and martyrologies (books containing a list of saints' names with their feast days). Not all of them tally in terms of dates and events, which means that we have no agreed version of St Bronagh's origins, life or death. As a result, hard facts have often been replaced by stories which have not always been supported by documentation.

There are four pieces of physical evidence surviving today which relate, in theory at least, to St Bronagh, although all four date from several hundred years after her death: the old church in Kilbroney Cemetery; what is referred to as St Bronagh's bell; the High Cross in Kilbroney Cemetery and what has become known as St Bronagh's well.

The remains of the church in the old cemetery have been dated as being built any time from the 12th to the 15th Centuries. It possibly occupies the same footprint as an older wooden church, which may have existed at the time of Bronagh. The second is what is known as St Bronagh's Bell, although it apparently dates from at least 300 years after her death, judging by its shape. The bell is housed in St Mary's Star of the Sea Church, Rostrevor. Thirdly, the High Cross in the old cemetery beside the Church probably dates from the Ninth Century, which makes it about the same age as the bell. As with the church and bell, there is no direct evidence to link the cross to St Bronagh during her lifetime.

The final piece of evidence is what is referred to as St Bronagh's Well. It is marked by a shrine in the cemetery. By examining local streams and ground water levels, it is hard to avoid the conclusion that what is now called the well, may not have been a well during the time of the first ecclesiastical settlement there. The rath on which the church was built most likely had a stream running along each side of it and these two streams may have supplied drinking water for the inhabitants. Where the well is today may have been more of a low-lying boggy area and the well may have been further North than the modern-day shrine. Only by examining such evidence can we achieve a more accurate understanding of St Bronagh's life and times.

Finally, there may have been one saint associated with the parish who is less well known than Bronagh. Killowen is the name given to six townlands to the Southeast of Rostrevor. Although traditionally translated as *Cill Eoghain*, meaning Eoin's or John's Church, there is no evidence of an Eoin or John in that area. However, the townland of Kilfeaghan in Killowen means the church of (Saint) Féichín. Directly visible from Kilfeaghan is the County Louth village of Termonfeichin (the refuge of Féichín) where the saint established a medieval monastery in the 7th Century. So, if there was a church built by, or associated, with St Féichín, why is the area called Killowen?

The answer may lie in common pronunciation where older people to this day refer to "Kill-oughwan" which would appear to be an anglicisation of *Cill Abhainn*, the church of/at the river. A recent survey by local historians in Kilfeaghan established an area known as Shankill (*sean cill* meaning "old church") close to the Cassy Water River in Kilfeaghan. There may have been more than one saint with an influence in the parish of Kilbroney. St Féichín may have had a say here too.

What is known as St Bronagh's Bell, on the wall of the old church.

CHAPTER 3

The New Beliefs

Christianity effectively marks the beginning of Irish history in that it offers comprehensive written records for the first time. The standard texts on the introduction of Christianity into Ireland state that St Patrick arrived here as a missionary in 432. The accuracy of the date cannot be guaranteed and while historical details on his activities in South Down are scarce, he is reputedly buried in Downpatrick. Although a large granite stone marks his apparent grave in the town, it was only placed there in the early 20th Century to prevent pilgrims taking handfuls of soil from the site.

The claim that he was buried at that spot is influenced by what might be called 12th Century propaganda by the Anglo-Norman, John de Courcy. Understanding the deep-rooted appeal of the cult of relics and the important role of saints as patrons to the local people, de Courcy staged the "discovery" of the relics of saints Brigit, Colum Cille and Patrick in 1185. He reportedly exhumed their bodies and transferred the relics into a new tomb at Downpatrick[1]. Despite that, it is generally believed that St Patrick is buried somewhere in or near Downpatrick. Before the arrival of his remains there, tradition has it that his body spent the last night of the journey to Downpatrick in Kilcoo (*Cill Chua*, "church of parting sorrow").

Saint Bronagh

The most prominent Christian figure in Rostrevor was not St Patrick, but St Bronagh, who reputedly died in 512 and about whom we have little authenticated knowledge: "Of the history of this saint we know practically nothing."[2] There is no evidence to suggest whether she belonged to this area or arrived from somewhere else. If she came from elsewhere, there is no evidence to indicate how, when or why she came here. There are several attempted explanations of her ancestry and family, none of them particularly reliable, since much of what has been described about her was written several centuries after her death.

The main source of information about Bronagh (original Irish spelling *Brónach*, meaning 'sorrowful')[3] comes from various biographies and martyrologies (books containing a list of saints' names with their feast days). Not all of them tally in terms of dates and events, which means that we have no agreed version of St Bronagh's origins, life or death. As a result, hard facts have often been replaced by made-up versions of her life which, while offering a convenient story-line, have done little to add to our knowledge or understanding. Only by examining the available evidence today can we achieve a more accurate appreciation of St Bronagh's life and times.

Most sources agree that the name "Kilbroney" is derived from its patron saint: "Bronach, a virgin of Seichis Church," *(Brónoch, Ógh, ó Chill Sechis)*[4] whose feast day is April 2. Legend suggests that she was killed by Vikings, but this is unlikely because, if the date of her arrival here is correct, she was dead for about 300 years before they arrived in Ireland. (See Chapter 4). It is also unlikely that she offered a refuge for shipwrecked sailors, since Carlingford Lough is particularly well sheltered from the worst excesses of the weather. Tradition suggests that she had a brother, Gall (not Saint Gall) who became a priest and later a bishop with his See in the Dromore area.[5] It is claimed that he built the monastery for his sister and gave her his staff. So she became the only female Irish saint to carry a staff.

Fig 3.1 *The old church on the site of what may have been St Bronagh's original church in Kilbroney Valley.*

O'Clery's references to her were written more than 1,000 years after her death, although they claim to be based on older references. They state that she was the daughter of Miliuc, son of Buan, with whom St Patrick was in captivity[6] and that she had two sons: Caolán[7] and Colman of Uisneach (Westmeath)[8]. Another source suggests that she was the daughter "of the petty king Miliuc of Dál nAraidi/Dál mBúain whom [St] Patrick served as a slave"[9], that she had a son called Fursa and that she was also the mother of Saint Mo Chóe of Nendrum (Mahee Island in Strangford Lough).

However, if Bronagh belonged to roughly the same generation as St Patrick in the fifth/sixth century and Fursa was not born until the sixth/seventh century, St Bronagh is unlikely to have been his mother. Indeed it has been pointed out that if we were to take everything written in the medieval period at face value, St Bronagh's children were fathered by four different men, with their birthdates covering more than one generation.[10]

This is obviously fiction and one explanation is that it is not concerned with the saint as a historical person, but is an attempt to trace various other saints back to St Patrick to give them religious authenticity. While there may have been an element of truth in what was written, there was also a degree of creativity to suit the trends in political and ecclesiastical developments during the medieval period in which most of them were written. As a result we have little reliable information about St Bronagh. This is not to suggest that there was no Saint Bronagh, it simply means that any description of her is based on an oral tradition rather than written evidence.

The Martyrology of Tallaght gives her feast day as April 2,[11] but offers no further information. She is also referred to as *Bronach uirgo o Glinn Sechis*[12] and another martyrology states that she had a son called Bute.[13] T. M. Charles-Edwards points out[14] that "female saints were relatively common east of the Bann but their cults were, on the whole, only of local significance. A good example is Brónach (5th–6th cent.?) of Kilbroney, whose feast day is 2 April. Her church, Cell Brónche, became the parish church of Glenn Sechis, the valley running down to Rostrevor. The old church was sufficiently important to be marked by a high cross. To judge by similar churches elsewhere, Cell Brónche and Dún dá Én are likely to have been founded as nunneries—or, at least, churches served by one or more nuns—but were also pastoral centres with a priest or priests attached."

Among the female saints were Saint Bridget, associated with Faughart in North Louth and Saint Monnina in Killeavy, South Armagh. Former Irish Primate, Cardinal Tomás O Fiaich has written that "The cult of local patron saints has remained very much alive in this area until the present day, and a generation ago exiles from the district were wont to pray:

A Bhríd atá i bhFochairt
A Bhlinne atá i gCill Shléibhe
A Bhrónaigh atá in mBaile na Cille
Go dtuga sigh mise go hEirinn."[15]

(Translation: Bridget who is in Faughart, Moninna who is in Killeavy, Bronagh who is in the town/home/place of the church, may you bring me to Ireland".)

An early historical reference to Bronagh (in English and Irish)[16] describes her as Brónach beoda (lively Brónach) which would appear at odds with the sorrowful implication of her name. The English translation in the text describes her as "vivacious Bronach" (which perhaps has a different modern meaning) and *ógh, ó Ghlinn Sechis* (a virgin from Glen Sechis). It is difficult to establish how accurate this description might be, since the Martyrology was composed in the latter part of the 12th century by Marianus Gorman, abbot of the Hills of the Apostles monastery at Knock, "close to the town of Louth"[17]. It was transcribed about 1630 by one of the Four Masters, Michael O'Clery.

Prior to the emergence of the place name, Kilbroney, the valley was generally referred to as *Glenn Seichis*, a form attested not only in Irish but also in Latin documents of the late medieval period where it appears in Anglicized form. That it is to be identified with Kilbroney is clear from the Papal Taxation of 1306, where it is stated to be in the diocese of Dromore (*Eccles. Tax.* 114), and from the Irish sources where it is associated with *Saint Brónach*. Although the word *seichis* is of unknown origin, Mooney[18] believes that it may 'be based on the Old-Irish word *sech* sometimes used as a prefix meaning 'secluded', and that *Glenn Seichis*, therefore, might mean 'glen of seclusion'.

However, the use of the word *gleann* (valley) is rare in the Mournes. The exception is Glenloughan, a townland just across the Cassy Water which marks Kilbroney parish's Eastern boundary. Its origin is actually *Cluain Lochán*, where the *cluain* (meadow) replaces *gleann*. Just across the Moygannon River, which marks the parish's Western boundary is *Cluain Dalláin* - Clonallon (Saint) Dallan's meadow. Could *Glenn Seichis* have been *Cluain Seichis*, meaning a secluded or possibly a sheltered meadow?

Whereas the old name *Glenn Seichis* lingered on in the records until the 17th century, Kilbroney was referred to by a number of names at different points in history including Glentegys (possibly from *Gleann Seichis*), Nister (possibly a corruption of *Diseart*, meaning a desert, since the earlies Christian monasteries were founded in deserts)[19] Clonfeys, Clonseys (both of which may come from *Cluain Seichis*, as opposed to *Gleann Sechis*) and Kyllbronca. Kilbroney appears to have become the standardised version of the name from the 14th Century, as evidenced by a reference in 1306 to, "The Church of Glentegys, otherwise of Nister.....now the parish of Kilbroney".[20] "Kilbroney" is presented in a variety of spellings in various civil and ecclesiastical documents and maps from the 14th to the 19th Centuries, before the current spelling was universally adopted.

What appears to be its Anglicised form still survives in Killowen, where Broney's well was marked on OS maps up to the 1930s in the townland of Ballinran. Whether this had any direct connection to St Bronagh is unknown. It may just have been an attempt to replicate the Kilbroney well or, if St Bronagh arrived by sea, it may have been her first place of residence before moving to Kilbroney. It was certainly a more likely location to offer help to sailors seeking refuge.

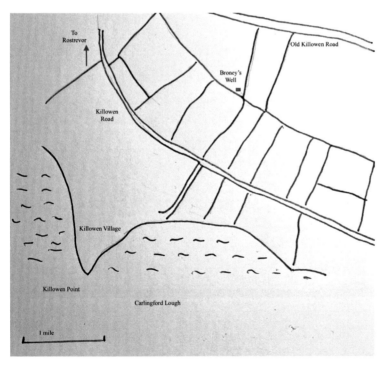

Fig 3.2 Sketch map with approximate field boundaries, showing the location of Broney's Well, as on the Ordnance Survey Second Edition Maps, 1846-1862.

Some time before October 1608, there was a request by Catherine Magennis (d 1619)[21], for a papal indulgence for three churches in Iveagh in the Diocese of Dromore[22]: Seapatrick, Saints Philip and James in Cluandallan (Clonallon) and "St Bronagh in Leggan". MacCuarta writes that "Leggan" probably refers to Kilbroney. In 1567 a Captain John Sankeye received property in "the barony of Legan in the Magennis country".[23] Legan may come from the Irish word lógan meaning a low-lying place, which could apply either to Kilbroney or Killowen.

However, the origin of the word remains unclear, particularly in view of its context in the original Latin: "Pro Ecclesia Sanctae Broivianae de [L]eggan nuncupata Dromorensis diocesis…". Mac Cuarta points out: "Magennis patronage may have helped preserve the shrine of St Bronagh at Kilbroney, for friar Edmund MacCana, writing in 1644, noted that 'at [her] statue God has performed many miracles in our day'.[24] It is not known where her statue stood at that time. In the absence of reliable written records, the only evidence in support of St Bronagh lies in identifying physical objects which have survived to this day. There are four pieces of evidence, although all four date from periods long after St Bronagh is believed to have existed: the old church in Kilbroney Cemetery; what is referred to as St Bronagh's bell; the High Cross in Kilbroney Cemetery and what is known as St Bronagh's well.

The Old Church

The old stone church has been identified in the previous chapter as being sited in a rath. One source has suggested that the current stone building, dates from the 12th century, probably replacing an original 6th Century wooden building on the same rectangular base.[25] Another argues that the church is "evidently 15th century" in origin.[26] The church is perfectly aligned East-West, which raises the question as to whether it is based on the same footprint as the original wooden structure. It would have been difficult in the early Christian era to determine compass directions accurately and the positions of sunrise and sunset in the valley would have been of little help.

The present church was originally a rectangular, gabled building about 13.3 metres by 6.2 metres, with walls about 1 metre thick. At a later date a chancel[27] was added (on the side towards the river) presumably as a reserved space for the clergy near the altar. It is 5.9 metres by 5 metres with walls about 0.7 metres thick. (Fig 3.4)

Fig 3.3 What is referred to as St Bronagh's Church in Kilbroney Old Cemetery.

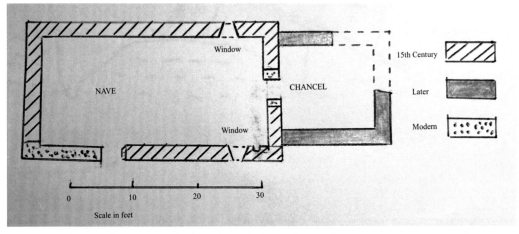

Fig 3.4 Sketch diagram of the church based on the 1966 Ministry of Finance Archaeological Survey plan, which suggests that the church dates from the 15th Century.

When the chancel was added, the stone masons did not tie it into the existing walls by replacing some existing stones with new connecting ones to join the two walls together. Instead they just abutted it against the existing building. (Fig 3.5) which suggests a reluctance to disturb the stones in the existing church wall. Whether this was for religious or structural reasons is not clear. The same technique was used to build a buttress against the south-facing wall. The builders may have used hidden stone riveting, whereby two pieces of stone are joined together by connecting a hole in each piece with another stone, but that is structurally less effective.

There are the remains of a small building to the west of the Church (about 10 metres towards the road) which may have been a shrine built at the time of the church. It now has two slate headstones in it. The west wall of the church (adjacent to the possible shrine) is probably one of the original pieces of the early church.

The window facing up the valley is also original. The other one, facing towards the Lough, is original but it has been repaired, as evidenced by the thin head lintel. The upper part of this wall probably collapsed in the 1800s, which is when the head of the window was rebuilt.

Fig. 3.6 Possible shrine to the West of the church.

74

Fig 3.7 Original window in the wall facing up the valley.

Fig 3.8 Window facing the lough with the head lintel as part of its repair. Through the opening we can see the window in the wall facing up the valley, which is in its original state.

The roof was probably thatched originally, because the span was too big to support the weight of shingles. The original wall plate discovered during restoration suggests that the roof had a very high pitch. The entrance was probably originally in the Southern wall (facing the river) but it has been altered. The two long windows (evidenced by the two arches in the wall, (Fig 3.9) originally extended down for about 2 metres each.

At some point after the15th Century a big wide doorway was punched through this wall (as evidenced by the arch) and the chancel outside the door was added on. The doorway is now much smaller, possibly because the big entrance weakened the structure of the wall. The windows may have been closed up for the same structural reason, probably in the 1500s. An alternative explanation may be that the arches were simply a building technique to strengthen the walls, although this is not common in buildings of this age in Ireland. The small square recess in the side wall near the southern entrance was probably used for religious objects[28]. The original plasterwork of the building was discovered in the built-up windows during restoration. A fragment of carved stone which was found along the North wall of the church during restoration may be the top of a font.

Fig 3.10 Recess in the side wall.

By the 1640s the site had been abandoned. Since there were few stone buildings in Ireland at this time, the English would have regarded the church as a possible stronghold, so they

probably burned the roof to render the building useless. Associated with the church is St Bronagh's staff, which was reportedly found there in the early 1800s. It appears to have been like 3 cylindrical candle sticks joined together, made of bronze with wooden shafts in the interiors. The wood was apparently burned at some point.

More accurately described as St Bromana's *baculus* or crozier, it was assigned by the bishop of the diocese to a clerical keeper and in 1427 the Bishop appointed Agholy McDermydan to be"custos baculi sanct Bromanae, Dromorensis Dioc" (keeper of the staff of S. Bronach, Diocese of Dromore).[29] The tradition of carrying a staff appears to have extended to wider society. An observer in the 12th Century noted that the Irish "have a great reverence for bells that can be carried about, and staff belonging to the saints, made of gold and silver, or bronze, and curved at their upper ends."[30] The crozier appears to have been entrusted to the custody of the Mercy nuns in more modern times, but its current whereabouts is unknown and it has not survived as a physical artefact. It has been suggested that the crozier is in the National Museum in Dublin,[31] but the Museum failed to confirm this.

The Bell

The second surviving remnant from the early medieval period is what is referred to as St Bronagh's Bell, although it apparently dates from about 300 years after her death. Its exact date of origin is unclear, but it was probably made some time around 800 AD or slightly later. Most early medieval bells are housed in museums, but three are the property of Catholic parishes: Omagh, Rostrevor and Culdaff.[32] The earliest bells in the Irish Christian tradition were made of hammered sheet iron, riveted on two sides, quadrangular in form, sloping from the base upwards to the crown, and surmounted by a handle. They were then dipped in a solution of molten bronze, which filled up all the apertures and coated the bell, giving it more resonance and solidity.

The quadrangular shape continued until about the twelfth century, with the angles, gradually becoming more rounded, until the round shape was eventually adopted.[33] They were rung by striking them with a hammer or small mallet. It is not clear how what is called St Bronagh's Bell was manufactured. Damage to the handle reveals an iron core, but this may not be the original handle and in the absence of detailed scientific analysis, the date and manufacturing process of the bell will remain uncertain. The bell itself is just over 10 inches high and its mouth measures about 7 inches square.

In 1903, the antiquarian S F Milligan wrote, "I was shown this bell by the Rev Mr Lowry CC in the church in the year 1888. It is a fine specimen of a bronze bell. Father Lowry gave me the following particulars: - It was found about a century ago among the branches of a tree that had been blown down during a storm, in the ruins of the monastery of St Broncha, patroness of the parish."[34] The traditional story in Rostrevor is that the bell was hidden in a tree for safekeeping (possibly at the same time as the roof was burned) and that it remained there for so long that its existence was forgotten about. On stormy nights a bell could be heard ringing, but its location was not revealed until the tree blew down in a storm. Prior to its removal from the church to a tree, the bell may have been housed in a recess high up in the gable nearest the road.

Fig 3.11 St Bronagh's Bell. The picture on the right shows where a small tear has been repaired. It was possibly caused by repeated striking on the same spot. Altar servers in Rostrevor were told to always strike the repaired section during Mass, even though it gave a slightly higher pitch than the lower portion of the bell.

Fig 3.12 Recess in the gable wall which may have housed the bell.

Fig 3.13 The wooden frame (left) with the bell in place (right).

According to the Newry Register of 1815, "this ancient bell was found a considerable time previously in the ivy surrounding the ruined church in which it had lain concealed until dislodged by a violent storm. The finder appears to have carried it to Newry, since in the year mentioned above it is stated to have been then in use as an altar bell in the Roman Catholic Church in that town." Subsequently it was transferred to the Catholic Church in Rostrevor where it was rung on the altar during Mass, hanging on a specially made wooden frame. In 1989 the bell was removed from the altar, which was being "modernized" and it was placed behind bars in a recess of the wall inside the Church. It is perhaps best viewed against the backdrop of Kilbroney Valley. (Fig 3.14)

Fig 3.14 The bell overlooking what might have been Cluain Seichis.

The High Cross

The third surviving piece of evidence about St Bronagh is the High Cross in Kilbroney Cemetery, which probably dates from around 800 AD.[35] It has been repaired at some point in the past. In 1966 it was described as being "extremely weathered".[36] It is described as "a monolithic unsigned cross of granite some two and a half metres tall, 30cm wide and over 18cm thick at the butt, narrowing to 28cm wide and 13 cm thick at the apex with an arm-span of 93 cm."[37] Only the west face of the cross (towards the road) is ornamented with a lozenge (diamond shape) at the centre of the cross-head.[38] Kelly argues that the overall impression of the cross is that it was originally conceived in three vertical segments, which suggests that it was first made of wood and then copied in stone. "A number of crosses in Ireland and Scotland can be shown to be related to this cross at Kilbroney, principally by the particular nature of the treatment of the hollowed angles at the junction of shaft and transom."[39]

Fig 3.15 High cross in Kilbroney old cemetery (left) with carving detail (right).

Cormac Bourke has identified four types of ancient Irish crosses: three of them have a ring normally associated with Celtic crosses and the fourth type has no ring: "The ringlets cross of type 4 is rare as a free-standing monument."[40] He points out that the Kilbroney cross bears an all over key-pattern ornament similar to that covering one face of the south cross at Castledermot, County Kildare and the two crosses are of similar proportion. The Kildare cross has been dated to the Ninth Century.

One of the closest crosses to Kilbroney in both form and in terms of geography is a cross at Clonlea, just 6 km from Kilbroney on the Grinan Lough Road. Although it is badly weathered, traces of the carvings can still be made out. The crosses at Kilbroney and Clonlea are regarded by Kelly as among the oldest in Ireland and mark the transition from wooden crosses to stone during the eighth century.[41]

Fig 3.16 Clonlea High Cross, Grinan.

The Well

The final relic of the early medieval period is what is known as St Bronagh's well, currently marked by a shrine. Like many holy wells, locals would attest to its curative properties for ailments of the eyes. It lay outside what was the perimeter of the rath, but there is some uncertainty regarding its status as a well. (It as referred to as St Bridget's well on the first OS map of 1832 and on some subsequent maps.)

Fig 3.17 The church which is associated with St Bronagh, with St Bronagh's well and shrine (top left).

Fig 3.18 The shrine at St Bronagh's well with the walls of the old church to the left in the background.

The evidence from geography and history, however, raises questions about the belief that the well was the rath's and later the monastery's source of water (or at least their sole source of water). It is more likely that water was supplied by one and possibly two streams, which were re-directed from their original routes in the 18th and/ or 19th Centuries. The original water supply for the rath probably came from the stream known today as Bandy Bridge (named after the shape of the bridge on the Kilbroney Road).

The reason for this assumption is that the water course has been artificially straightened from before it crosses under Kilbroney Road down to where Martin's house and mill stood at the Green (Fig 3.19). Using what is known as hydromorphological analysis, the most likely course for Bandy Bridge stream would have been towards the rath where the Church was later built. This would have been a potential source of water for the rath and later for the ecclesiastical settlement. That course would also have brought the stream alongside a now disappeared rath at the edge of the Kilbroney Road (Fig. 2.15)

Fig 3.19   The white line indicates the likely original course of Bandy Bridge from Levallyclanone to the Kilbroney River, passing the rath and later the monastic site. The red straight line indicates the straightened course of the stream to suit Martin's house and/or mill.

The second stream which probably supplied the rath and the later monastic settlement flowed through the grounds of Leacain House, now called Mourne Wood. Originally it most likely flowed down from Levallyclanone and went under what became Kilbroney Road somewhere near the entrance gates to the Council cemetery. When the Martin family built Leacain House in the 19th Century, the stream was modified as it passed through its grounds. On reaching Kilbroney Road it was diverted through 90 degrees to its right, flowing as an open channel directly beside the road towards Rostrevor. It then passed under the road at what is now Shanowen, just as it does today.

Before it was diverted, it is likely to have flowed down towards where St Bronagh's well is today, passing the monastery on its Southern side, just as the Bandy Bridge stream passed it on the Northern side. So the original rath would have been sited between two fresh water supplies, which were later used by the monastic settlement. Whether there was a well there in St Bronagh's time is difficult to determine. It may have become one after the stream from Leacain House was diverted. In modern times the lower portion of the cemetery below the shrine was often waterlogged.[42]

In the 1980s and 1990s, the stream from Leacain House was piped to accommodate a new housing development at what is now Mourne Wood. As a result, the level of the water table fell in the lower half of the cemetery and the level of the well dropped significantly to the point where a hand pump was installed to force water to the surface. The question therefore arises as to whether this was a well or merely a soak-away from higher ground at or above the road.[43] If it had been a soak-away, it may have been an area for animals rather than humans to drink. If there was a well in the monastic grounds for human use (in addition to the two streams), it is likely to have been higher up the slope near the road. That would have been in keeping with the line of wells which ran along the Kilbroney Road, usually on the basis of one for every house.[44]

A functioning convent or monastery would have required more land than that contained within the rath where the old church now stands. The church would have been part of a much wider settlement, which probably extended up the Kilbroney valley for about half a mile, including what became the glebe land at Covernnestrade. (See Place-names section.) The physical extent of St Bronagh's monastic settlement is unknown, but it would have included not just the church, but associated buildings for domestic purposes, crops storage, food preparation, animal shelter and accommodation for various support workers on the site. So although Tullyfrenchy Well, for example, is a few hundred metres from the church ruins, it conceivably could have been within the extended monastic settlement. Of course, there may have been one well within the monastic site.

In all the graves I have seen dug in the cemetery, I have seen no evidence of any building materials, or foundations, although Sr Evelyn Kenny of the Mercy Convent in Newry indicates that when digging the foundations for the stone shrine at St Bronagh's well, "workmen discovered an altar stone bearing marks of early origin, probably belonging to the 7th or 8th Century."[45] Whatever its authenticity, what is referred to as St Bronagh's well has been of important religious significance in modern times, particularly because of its reputation as having a cure for illnesses of the eyes. In 1938 a stone shrine was erected over the well by Felix O'Hare and Co and it was opened and blessed by Bishop Mulhern on August 14, in what was an event of major social significance in the parish.[46]

Fig 3.20 Bishop Mulhern consecrating the shrine in 1938.

Fig 3.21 A section of the large crowd in attendance.

Saint Féichín

St Bronagh is not the only saint associated with Kilbroney parish. The area known as Killowen to the east of the parish, along and above the Northern shore of Carlingford Lough, is made up of eight townlands. The name "Killowen" is generally translated as Eoin's Church or possibly John's Church.[47] However, older people in the parish and certainly in Kilbroney, did not call it Killowen. They called it Kill-oughwan, which is close to the Irish, *Cill Abhainn*, meaning the Church of the River. There is a river, the Cassy Water, flowing down the side of Kilfeaghan, one of Killowen's eight townlands, which marks the boundary not only of Kilbroney parish, but of Dromore Diocese. So there certainly could have been a Church of/at the River.

This view is supported by Matthew Russell SJ who wrote[48] that "The old chapel [in Killowen] was never known by the name of any patron saint." The name of the townland Kilfeaghan would suggest that the church is named after St Féichín, a seventh century saint who founded a monastery at Fore in County Westmeath. This would have been about a century after the date attributed to St Bronagh. There is a high cross in the cemetery at Fore, which may be of the same age as St Bronagh's, although it is of a different style. So, could St Féichín have any connection with Kilfeaghan? Mooney does not think so.[49]

However, there is one obvious connection which he appears to have overlooked. Tradition has it that St Féichín founded a monastery in the Louth village of Termonfeckin (*Tearmann Féichín*, meaning Féichín's refuge), where there is also a high cross in the cemetery. The monastery was destroyed by the Vikings in 1013. The connection between Féichín's refuge in County Louth and Féichín's church in County Down is that on a clear day you can see one location from the other. This is not to suggest that it is possible to see one building from the other, but you can certainly see one townland from the other, a distance of just over 25 miles.

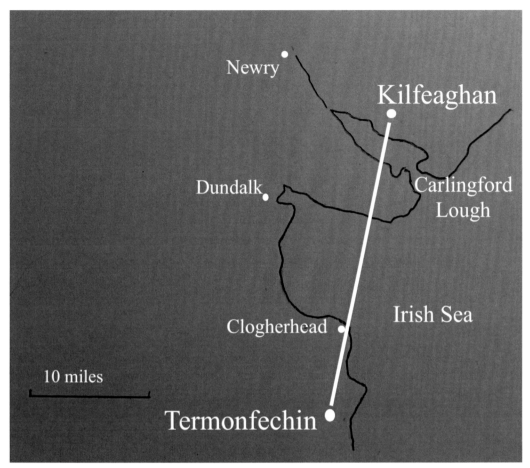

Fig 3.22 Line of sight between Kilfeaghan and Termonfechin.

Could it be that, while in Termonfeckin, St Féichín saw the South-facing slopes of the Mournes and decided to build a church there? Or did those who built the first church in Killowen name it in honour of the saint whose monastic site they could see, in general terms, from Kilfeaghan? Whether the name *Cill Abhainn* (Killowen) came before or after *Cill Feaghan* (Kilfeaghan) is not known. They may both refer to the same church. Mooney believes that the name Killowen is older, but he offers no evidence.[50] There probably never was a Church of Eoin. The reasoning lies in the landscape. Significantly, in May 2022 a historical group in Killowen researched place names in the area and in Kilfeaghan they identified a site known as Seanchill, meaning "old church", just a few hundred feet from the Cassy Water River.[51] That is where Cill Abhainn is most likely to have been, a point supported by Mooney.[52]

Kilfeaghan

Fig. 3.23 Kilfeaghan as seen from the Louth Coast just North of Termonfeckin. The mountain on the left is Slieve Foy and Carlingford Lough lies between it and Kilfeaghan.

Less than 400 years after St Patrick's arrival and as Christianity began to take root, the first Vikings invaded Ireland around 795 AD. They continued to invade and establish settlements until 1014. A pattern of invasion and colonisation from overseas had begun. It would continue for centuries and it would shape much of the Rostrevor area as we know it today. While the influence of these various invaders generally waned after a period, the original Christian influence outlived all of them. Christianity shaped Rostrevor more than any other influence during this period and its influence has persisted until the present day.

Chapter Endnotes

1   Wycherley N (2022) *St Patrick: just where is the saint's body?* RTE Brainstorm Podcast.
2   www.ucc.ie/celt/odonovan.html: Letters Written by John O'Donovan, pp 53-54.
3   The Church of Ireland in Rostrevor continues to use the Name Bronach, which is more original than Bronagh. See: Roberts S and Coffey P (2021) Celebrating 200 years of Saint Bronach's, Kilbroney Parish Church, Rostrevor.
4   O'Clery, M (1630) *Feilire na Naomh Nerennach, Martyrologium Dungallense*, P 92. Published by the Irish Archaeological and Celtic Society, 1863. References to the word *seichis* are not always consistent. It is sometimes spelt *sechis* as in this instance.
5   Letter to me from Sr Evelyn Kenny 24/02/2007 in the Mercy Convent, Newry.
6   O'Clery, p 1.
7   O'Clery, p 177.
8   O'Clery, p 259.
9   Hamann S (2012) St Fursa, the genealogy of an Irish saint- the historical person and his cult. *Proceedings of the Royal Irish Academy: Archaeology, Culture, History, Literature*, Vol 112 (2012) p 153.
10   Hamann, p 155.
11   Kelly M (1857) *Calendar of the Irish Saints, the Martyrology of Tallaght*, p xx.
12   Stokes W (1905) *The Martyrology of Oengus The Culdee*, critically edited from ten manuscripts with a preface, translation, notes and indices, London, p 110.
13   Stokes p 257.
14   Charles-Edwards T M (2004). Ulster, saints of (act. c. 400–c. 650), were the foci of religious life in the north of Ireland. *Oxford Dictionary of National Biography*.
15   O Fiaich T (1970) The Political and Social Background of the Ulster Poets, *Léachtaí Cholm Cille* 1970 Litríocht na Gaeilge, An Sagart Má Nuad pp 23-33.
16   Stokes W (1895) *The Martyrology of Gorman*, edited from a manuscript in the Royal Library Brussels, with a preface, translation, notes and indices. London, pp 68 – 69.
17   Stokes p viii (The writer may be referring to Knockbridge, which is about three miles from Louth village.)
18   Mooney B J (1950) *Place-names of Rostrevor*. Newry.
19   Mooney p 6.
20   Reeves W (1848) *Ecclesiastical Antiquities of Down, Conor and Dromore, consisting of a taxation of those diocese compiled in the year MCCCVI (1306)*, Dublin p 115.
21   Catherine was a daughter of Sir Hugh Magenis, Lord of Iveagh. She married Hugh O'Neill in 1598.
22   MacCuarta B (2008) Papal Privileges for Ulster Churches, 1608, *Seanchas Ardmhacha: Journal of the Armagh Diocesan Historical Society* Vol. 21/22, Vol. 21, no. 2 - Vol. 22, no. 1 (2007/2008), pp. 59-68.
23   O'Sullivan H (1997) The Magennis Lordship of Iveagh in the Early Modern Period, 1534 to 1691 in Proudfoot L (ed) *Down History ad Society*, Geography Publications, p 162.
24   MacCuarta p 62.
25   This information is based on a talk given by Liam McQuillan, NIEPA Archaeological Section, in Kilbroney Cemetery, July 27, 2012.
26   Ministry of Finance 1966 *An Archaeological Survey of County Down* p 130.
27   A chancel is the part of a church near the altar, reserved for the clergy and choir, and typically separated from the nave by steps or a screen/wall.
28   My father, Matthew Murphy, said locals always believed it was for keeping the water and the wine.
29   Atkinson E D (1829) *Dromore: An Ulster Diocese* p 70.
30   O'Meara J (translator) (1982)   Gerald of Wales Penguin, p 116.
31   Flanagan L (1990). *A Chronicle of Irish Saints*, Blackstaff Press Belfast p 46. I contacted the National Museum in early 2022 to ask if there was any evidence for the claim. They said they looked in their archives and could find no record of it.
32   *The ancient hand-bells that still ring true for every Christian faith on these islands* Irish Times February 5, 2021.
33   Milligan S F (1903) Ancient Ecclesiastical Bells in Ulster, *Society of Antiquaries Royal of Ireland*, Vol 33 No 1 p 46.
34   Milligan p 55.
35   Kelly D (1991) The Heart of the Matter: Models for Irish High Crosses, *Journal of the Royal Society of Antiquaries of Ireland* Vol 121 pp 142-143.
36   Ministry of Finance p 303.
37   Kelly p 109.
38   Richardson H (1996) *Lozenge and Logos Archaeology Ireland* Vol 10, No 2 p 24.
39   Kelly p 109.
40   Bourke C (1980) Early Irish Hand-bells. *The Journal of the Royal Society of Antiquaries of Ireland,* Vol 110 p 56.
41   Kelly pp142-3.
42   Certainly as a child I can remember that graves which were dug below the shrine were often filled with water by the time the burial took place.
43   Some graves in the new municipal cemetery can also become waterlogged along the line of what may have been the

stream from Leacain House. One gravedigger, on September 20, 2023, referred to it as "a vein of water" running down the hill.

44   I encountered a group of Travellers in a field further up Kilbroney Road from the cemetery in the 1990s. They said they were looking for St Bronagh's well and when I told them that it was in the cemetery, they replied that in their oral tradition, the well there was not St Bronagh's. The real well, they insisted, was further up Kilbroney Road. Thus St Bronagh's well may in fact have been the well which Kilbroney people know as Tullyfrenchy (probably *Tulach foinsí*, the low hill or mound of the spring).

45   Sr Evelyn Kenny letter

46   My father was a joiner who worked for O'Hare's for many years. He and others made the wooden casing for the stone masons to build the shrine's internal arch.

47   Mooney p 18.

48   Russell M (1912) *The Three Sisters of Lord Russell of Killowen and Their Convent Life* p 13.

49   Mooney p 19.

50   Mooney p 18.

51   Rostrevor News Facebook Page, May 27, 2002.

52   Mooney p 18.

CHAPTER 4

Narrow Water Castle

Medieval Times

Carlingford Castle with Rostrevor in the background.

Chapter 4 Summary

Invaders and the Emergence of the Parish

The Medieval period covers the years roughly between 750 and 1550 AD. There were three main influences on Rostrevor during this time: the Vikings, the Anglo-Normans and the Church.

The Vikings began a series of attacks in Ireland from about 800 AD onwards, initially along Ireland's East coast. There is no evidence of their having arrived in what became Rostrevor, but since they had a strong presence on Carlingford Lough, it is almost certain that they visited the coastal area where the village later grew up.

One of their main strongholds was at a place known as *Linn Duchaill* near Annagassan on the Southern shores of Dundalk Bay, which they developed from about 841 AD. From that location the Vikings could have clearly seen the Western Mournes overlooking Carlingford Lough, so they were certainly aware of the existence of the Rostrevor shoreline.

The name Carlingford is of Viking origin and other relics of their presence in the Rostrevor area include two common South Down surnames. In Irish the Vikings were known as *na Lochlannaigh* (singular *Lochlannach*), so the modern surname McLoughlin means son of a Viking. Another common name is Doyle which is derived from *Ó Dubhghaill* (the black foreigner) which is thought to refer to the darker-haired Danes as opposed to the more fair-haired Norwegians. The Vikings eventually merged with wider Irish society and their main legacy was founding the city of Dublin.

In 1169 another set of invaders arrived in Ireland: the Anglo-Normans. They were descendants of Vikings who had invaded Normandy in France. They later invaded England as Normans in 1066, when they defeated the Saxons and effectively took over England. A century later they invaded Ireland.

Two years after landing in Ireland they had taken over major settlements including Dublin. In 1177, John de Courcy, a knight from Somerset, marched North from Dublin. Within four days, having marched through South Down on their way, they had reached Downpatrick, where their military superiority allowed them to defeat the native Irish in two significant battles.

The following year the battles continued between the invaders and the Irish, including at the Clanrye River (which flows through Newry) which the Irish won. They defeated the Anglo-Normans again close to Rostrevor at a battle at Narrow Water in 1211.

As part of the Anglo-Norman conquest, they built two castles and a keep (a fortified tower) on the shores of Carlingford Lough: Carlingford Castle, Greencastle and Narrow Water, where the keep was later replaced by a castle. Although there is no direct evidence of the Anglo-Normans in what became Rostrevor, they had a strong presence in South Down and on Carlingford Lough.

The final influence in this period is the Church, which certainly had a presence in Rostrevor. It was the time when the parish was first given the name Kilbroney to replace the older names Glentegys and Clonseys, both corruptions of the name Glen Seichis or possibly Cluain Seichis. Throughout the medieval period the old Gaelic system was gradually being weakened in the face of the growing influence of the English system. In Rostrevor that was marked by the declining influence of the Magennis clan and their replacement by the Trevors.

The medieval period marks the end of an era in Rostrevor's history. New invaders, who would shape Ireland, were about to arrive and attempt to remove Rostrevor from its Gaelic heritage and tie it into closer union with Britain. A new era was about to begin.

The Vikings had a strong presence on Carlingford Lough, but they would have had difficulty landing in Rostrevor at low tide.

CHAPTER 4

Medieval Rostrevor

In Medieval times Rostrevor, like much of Ireland, was subject to three major influences: invasion by the Vikings, a later invasion by the Anglo-Normans and most significantly, the lasting impact of the Church.

The Vikings

In 795 the Vikings began their invasion of Ireland with attacks on Rathlin Island and Lambay Island off the Dublin coast, as a prelude to more concerted attacks across the island. By 824 they were raiding County Down: "they plundered Bennchur of Uladh [Bangor] and brake the shrine of Comhghall and killed its bishop and its doctors, and its clergy: they devastated also the plain *Mag Mhbili*" (Movilla, Newtownards.)[1] "Lann Léiri [Dunleer, Co Louth] also, and Cenn Slebhi [Killeavy] were plundered by another party of them"[2] These attacks were related to the Vikings' journey to *Snámh Aigneach* (fast flowing sea channel) which is the old name for Carlingford.[3] (The modern name, Carlingford, is a Scandinavian name *kerling* ('hag') and *fjord* (narrow inlet of the sea between cliffs or steep slopes).[4]

If the Vikings arrived at Carlingford, they obviously were present on Carlingford Lough and were thus familiar with both its shorelines. There is no evidence they landed in what became Rostrevor, which at that time may have been little more than a few dwellings at the ford of the Kilbroney River (at the bottom of present-day Water Street) and possibly a small settlement at what is now the Quay.

However, it is unlikely that they landed on the Lough's Southern shore while ignoring its Northern side. It is not clear if the religious community still existed at St Bronagh's Church in Kilbroney. If it did, it would almost certainly have been plundered, since in 832, Armagh was plundered "by the heathens three times in one month."[5] Almost a century later, Vikings from Carlingford Lough plundered "one of the most important early nunneries in Ireland"[6], founded by St Moninna at Killeavy on the Eastern foot of Slieve Gullion. So until we can find some hard evidence to the contrary, we can reasonably assume by association that the Vikings had some contact with what became Rostrevor.

By 837, "A naval force of the Norsemen sixty ships strong was on the Bóinn" [River Boyne]"[7] In 840, "Lugbad [Louth] was plundered by the heathens from Loch nEchach [Lough Neagh] and they led away captive bishops and priests and scholars and put others to death."[8] If Louth was plundered, it is likely that South Down suffered the same fate. This is particularly true since what may have been the first Viking camp for over-wintering in Ireland, known as a *longphort* (plural *longphoirt*) was built at Annagassan on the Southern side of Dundalk Bay in 841. Known as *Linn Duchaill* (the pool of the demon) it was built at the same time as *Dubh Linn* (dark pool), which later became Dublin. Prior to the Viking invasion there appears to have been a monastery at Linn Duchaill (which may have attracted the raiders to the site).[9]

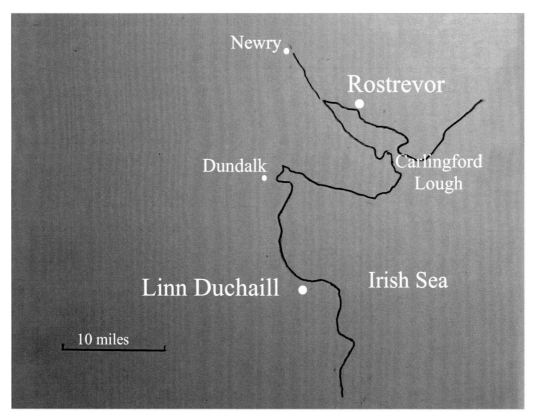

Fig 4.1 Map showing Linn Duchaill in context of Carlingford Lough and Rostrevor.

Linn Duchaill was a huge, fortified settlement up to 150 acres in size, where the Vikings built and repaired their ships, traded and raided into the surrounding countryside. It was in use for about 50 years continuously[10] and its relevance to Rostrevor is that, just as it was possible to see Kilfeaghan from Termonfeckin (about 9 miles South of Annagassan), it was possible to see the mountains near Rostrevor from Linn Duchaill.

The Vikings certainly knew our coastline and were therefore well acquainted with the area in the immediate vicinity of Rostrevor. Linn Duchaill was eventually abandoned in favour of using Dublin as a base. Dundalk Bay is shallow with a huge tidal range in Annagassan's Glyde River, which effectively meant that the Vikings were stranded upstream twice a day.

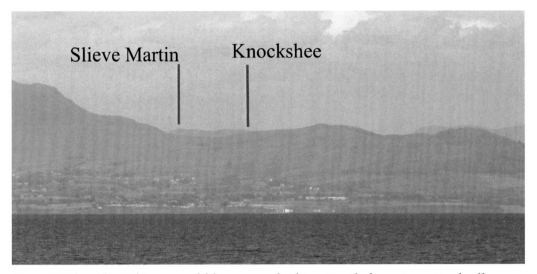

Fig 4.2 What the Vikings would have seen looking North from Linn Duchaill across Dundalk Bay. Slieve Foy is on the left.

The existence of Linn Duchaill suggests that there was no need for a Viking base in Carlingford Lough and there does not appear to be any physical evidence to support the existence of such a base.[11] There is a report[12] that in 828 the Vikings were slaughtering porpoises off the coast of County Louth for food. Fish were an important part of the Viking diet.

In 858, there was a naval battle between two groups of Vikings either in Carlingford Lough or just off the coast: "The complement of eight score ships of fair-haired foreigners came to *Snám Aignech* [Carlingford] to do battle with the dark foreigners; they fought for three days and three nights, but the dark foreigners got the upper hand and the others abandoned their ships to them."[13] (The reference to three days and three nights may simply mean a long period.) There is little evidence remaining today of the Viking influence on the Carlingford Lough area apart from some modern surnames which have a Norse origin. The Irish word for the Vikings is *Na Lochlannaigh* (singular *Lochlannach*) so that the son of a Viking is known today as McLoughlin[14] which is a common name in South Down. Another common name is Doyle which is derived from *Ó Dubhghaill* (the black foreigner) which is thought to have been used to distinguish the darker-haired Danes from the fairer-haired Norwegians.[15]

As the Vikings remained in Ireland, they became less hostile and although they continued to deal in wholesale slavery (as did the Irish at that time) they became more settled and developed trade and commerce with Irish chieftains. Indeed, it was the Vikings who founded what became Ireland's capital city, Dublin.

By 959 AD the Vikings had settled down in the lands they had conquered. They stopped raiding in Ireland and became involved in trading. For the next 100 years Ireland was relatively peaceful, but more invaders were on the way.

The Anglo-Normans

At about the same time as they invaded Ireland, the Vikings also invaded Normandy in Northern France in the 10th and 11th Centuries and settled there. They and their descendants became what were regarded as Normans and in 1066, they invaded England and ultimately ruled it. In 1169, now known as the Anglo-Normans, (they had been settled in England for over a century) they invaded Ireland, after "the Pope granted Ireland to the illustrious King of England, Henry, to be held by him and his successors".[16] Pope Adrian IV, the only English Pope, had issued a Papal Bull (a public edict) in 1155 giving Henry the authority to invade Ireland, so that he might bring the island more directly under the control of the Holy See.

The Anglo-Norman influence in South Down was particularly marked: "Outside of the central Pale, no part of the kingdom received so large an infusion of the early Anglo-Norman colonisation as Down, and none retained it so long and with so marked characteristics."[17] The Normans were particularly skilled in warfare and they had a remarkable ability to organise strong and efficient government.

Within two years of their landing in Ireland they had taken control of Dublin and Waterford and they then turned their attention to Ulster. In 1177, John de Courcy, a knight from Somerset, marched North from Dublin, "with only twenty-two men-at-arms and about three hundred others".[18] Within four days, having marched through South Down on their way, they had reached Downpatrick, where their military superiority allowed them to defeat the native Irish in two significant battles. "His route to Down in his first excursion was manifestly via Newry, Crown Bridge, Ballymaghery [Hilltown] and Clough".[19] As today, the main route from Newry to Downpatrick passed through Hilltown, rather than along the coastal route through Rostrevor.

There were a series of other military engagements between the Irish and the invaders. The nearest of these to Rostrevor were one at Narrow Water and another somewhere near Newry. In 1178, for example, the Annals of Ulster record that John [de Courcy] had been pillaging from Dun (presumably Downpatrick) to the Plain of Conaille (Dromiskin, County Louth) when they camped overnight at Glenn-righe, the old name for the Clanrye River.[20] The native Irish attacked them: "Thereupon defeat was inflicted upon the Foreigners and stark slaughter was put upon them".[21]

In 1211 "The Foreigners came to Narrow-Water, until Aedh Ua Neill assembled *Cenel-Conaill* ("the kindred of Conall" who were a branch of the O'Neill's) and *Cenel-Eogain* ("Eogain's kindred, another branch of the O'Neill's) and the Airghialla (Oriel today, covering South East Ulster and adjoining areas of Louth) so that the Foreigners were killed by him."[22] Another account states: "The English came to *Cael-uisge* (Narrow Water). Hugh O'Neill and Donnell O'Donnell, assembling their forces, marched thither, and slew the English, together with Henry Beg, and distributed their goods and property among their troops."[23]

Again, although there is no direct historical evidence to link the Anglo-Normans to Rostrevor, they certainly lived and fought very close to it. However, having largely conquered Ulster, de Courcy fell out of favour with the new English King John who, on his accession to the throne in 1199, authorised Hugh de Lacy to wage war against de Courcy. By 1205 de Lacy was Earl of Ulster. Five years later, however, he too fell out of favour and in 1210 King John arrived in Ireland with an army of 7,000 to ensure that all his nobles in Ireland carried out the royal will.

Fig 4.3 Narrow Water Castle at low tide.

Two castles and a keep (fortified tower) were built near Rostrevor around this time. All three were located along the shores of Carlingford Lough: Greencastle, St John's Castle in Carlingford and a keep at Narrow Water, where a castle from a later date now stands. All three were built at defensive strategic points on the Lough. Because Rostrevor was in a bay with a high tidal range, it was not suitable for defensive purposes and, in any case, it was at the widest point of the inlet.

De Lacey is thought to have built the keep at Narrow Water[24]: "A hosting by the Connachtmen, through summons of the Foreign bishop and of Gillibert Mac Coisdealbh, to Eas-ruadh, so that the castle of Narrow-Water was made by them."[25] The following year, "Gillibert Mac Coisdealbh was killed in the castle of the Narrow-Water and the castle was also burned at the time."[26]

Fig 4.4. Greencastle at the mouth of Carlingford Lough at low tide. The Irish Sea is in the background on the right.

Fig 4.5 Greencastle

The main period of construction at Greencastle can probably be dated between 1227 and 1242.[27] It has been described as "the best example of fully developed 13th Century military architecture" in County Down.[28] It became the centre of a manor with a church, the remains of which (or of a successor), stand in ruin in a field below the castle.[29] As well as its defensive role in supporting nearby Dundrum further along the coast, it also played a social role in providing accommodation for various nobility and military personnel on their way to and from Dublin, via a ferry to Carlingford. For a short time it was a new township, but it soon declined in importance.[30]

Fig 4.6 Carlingford Castle

When Carlingford Castle was built around 1190 by Hugh de Lacy II, his extended family owned about one third of all Norman land in Ireland.[31] However, the family were among those whom King John felt were not paying him due homage, so when he arrived in Ireland in 1210, he chased Hugh de Lacy II out of his earldom.[32] Although the castle is known as King John's Castle, his only significant connection with it appears to be the fact that he visited it in 1210 and stayed there for two days.

His association with the castle may be because he drove de Lacy out of it and made some repairs to it. This castle was built on a large rocky promontory which lies at the mouth of Carlingford Lough at the foot of Slieve Foy, giving it a naturally strategic location for defence. It may also have been chosen because it lies on the borderline of Leinster and Ulster, therefore protecting a possible entrance-way for the Ulster clans into this Anglo-Norman colony.

As well as their military domination, the Anglo-Normans also began to organise the structure of civil administration by introducing counties and baronies[33]. To govern Ireland they adopted the system they already had in England, by dividing the country into shires or counties, initially in Munster and Leinster. Subsequent English administrations continued this pattern.

Many of the new counties cut across existing Irish territorial divisions and although some of them were later ignored, they were resurrected during later plantations in Munster and Ulster. County Down was formed in the early 16th Century. Counties were then sub-divided, also following the English system, into baronies. These were not so much administrative divisions, but more what is termed a cadaster. This is an area in which property ownership is recorded. Rostrevor was in Iveagh Upper[34] which in 1851 was further divided into an upper and lower half. Rostrevor was located in the Upper half.

The Anglo-Norman hold on East Ulster weakened from about 1320 onwards as the Irish and the invaders slowly came together. The Magennis clan moved back into the once royal castle in Dundrum and although many Anglo-Normans became quite like the Irish in customs and habit, some of the Irish adapted the English ways too: in 1586 one of the Magennises was living and dressing "Englishe-like in his house at Rathfriland".[35] The Anglo-Norman legacy today can be seen in the physical landscape in the form of castles, but a more lasting impact has been the system of counties which formed the basis of English administration here for the following centuries.

The Church

While foreign invasions were shaping Ireland, a more lasting influence came from within. The major impact on Ireland came from the Church, which not only taught morals, but largely determined the nature and content of Irish social behaviour. This period marked the end of the monastic organisation of the Irish Church and the emergence of the modern parish system, which had its origins in the old Gaelic *tuath*, meaning a territorial unit. The Anglo-Normans used this as a basis for administration, mainly in the form of taxation, and they eventually evolved into civil parishes.[36] Although these were used as the basis for Church of Ireland parishes, the Catholic Church based its parishes on a system of towns and villages following the Reformation.[37]

The parish of Kilbroney was known by several names at various times in the past.[38] The names identified all come from official state or church sources, but whether these were the same names as used by the local Irish is not clear. In the Taxation of 1306, it is described as "The Church of Glentegys otherwise Nister," and is taxed at one mark.[39] Sixty years later it is referred to as Kyllwronaygh, when the Bishop of Dromore cited his clergy to appear there during what was called a metropolitical visitation planned for November 1366 in the place known as Kyllbronaygh: *in loco qui dicitur Kyllbronaygh.* [40]

The names Glentegys and Clonseys are both corruptions of the name Glen Seichis (sometimes referred to as Glenseichis). "Seichis" does not appear to be a modern Irish word, so its original meaning has been lost. It may refer to a secluded area[41], hence its relationship with *Nister*, which appears to have been derived from the old Irish *disert*, meaning a desert or a place of seclusion. It is not clear why there should have been two names, but one possible explanation is that Kilbroney may have referred to the actual site of the church (*cill* in Irish) and its suggested founder. The other may have applied to the wider area of the valley (*Gleann Seichis* or possibly *Cluain Seichis* in Irish). Whatever the explanation, by 1450 Kilbroney was the accepted name for the parish and the townland, although its spelling often varied.

Kilbroney was "of old, a mensal of the Bishop of Dromore"[42] meaning that "in the parish of *Kilbrony* the bishop had a mensal, consisting of certain lands, tithes, and dues, which were appendant upon the *Officium baculi sanctae Bromanae in ecclesia S. Bromanae* and were farmed by the ecclesiastic who was appointed by the bishop *custos baculi S. Bromanae*." St Bromana is called *Bronach* in the Irish calendar, feast day at the 2nd of April, and from her the parish derived its name. Her *baculus* or crozier seems to have been a relic which was preserved and was attended with specific privileges to the person responsible for keeping it.[43]

Officium baculi sanctae Bromanae in ecclesia S. Bromanae[44], meant that the staff of St Bronagh was associated with the church, either literally in that it was still held there, or that a relic of it had survived several hundred years after Bronagh's death. The local bishop appointed a cleric to the church as the custodian of St Bronagh's staff and he had certain privileges. His main obligation was responsibility for farming on church lands to raise money for the bishop. The land to the right-hand side of the upper entrance into Mourne Hall (across the road from the old cemetery gate) known as Covernnestrade was glebe land or tithe land, meaning that one tenth of its annual produce or income was taken as a tax for the support of the Church. Whether that was a continuation of the mensal system or a more recently introduced tax is unclear.

The custody of St Bronagh's "baculus" or staff was seemingly the title by which the person keeping it was given by the Bishop. The post of keeper does not appear to have been continuously occupied throughout the fourteenth and fifteenth centuries. Among those who held the position were:

> c 1427: Agholy Mcdermydan[45];
>
> January 1428: Master John Mcgerywey, Canon of Dromore;

August 1428: Gyllabrony McKewyn;

1431: Philip McKewyn

1433, the church of *Kilbrony* granted to John Mcgillaboy;

1442, Nov. 16, Clemens Mcdonnogan vicar of *Cillbronaid*.

1442 Nov. 17, the rectories of *Kyllbronca* and Dissertdubunnugi were let to farm to John Mcgillaboy, Canon of Dromore, for a term of five years, at 20s per year.

1526, the bishop's mensal of *Kilbrony*, held by Arthur Mcganyse, son of Gelacius, for two years, at four marks per annum.

From Patrick MacBrun in 1534 to Edward Floyd in 1630 (after which the succession is complete), the name of no vicar remains on record, so that for almost a hundred years the ecclesiastical history of the parish is a blank.

A list showing the income values for the Dromore parishes does not include Kilbroney in 1422, although it is listed as one of the diocese's 23 parishes.[46] Most parishes had two priests who were called a rector and vicar and although we have no idea of the cost of living at that time, their incomes suggest that priests were particularly poor. Most of Dromore's priests came from a small number of what are known as erenagh[47] families, meaning they had been associated with the church for centuries. Their names included Maginnis, McBrune, McGuirin, McKinnevin and O'Rooney.[48] A significant number of Dromore priests were titled *magister*, which indicates that they were university graduates. Although they were poor, they were well educated.

Many of them were also married, usually in a civil rather than a church ceremony. Although against canon law, civil marriage was a common practice across medieval Europe. Several were the sons of priests and, in turn, the fathers of priests.[49] Although the diocese of Dromore dates from the end of the twelfth century, it was without a bishop for most of the fifteenth and sixteenth centuries[50] and it was generally regarded as the Cinderella of the Northern dioceses.

As a result it came under the direct supervision of the archbishop of Armagh.[51] "In the fifteenth century, a great many bishops of this See lived, for the most part, in England, and spent little or none of their time in the government of their flock," mainly because of the poverty of the diocese.[52] Thus there were very often long vacancies in the diocese. Reeves (1847) lists Dromore's bishops from St Patrick in 493 up to 1200, compiled mainly from the Annals of the Four Masters. There is no mention of St Bronagh or any other convents or monasteries during that period. That is not to say they did not exist. They may have, but their existence was not officially recorded.

About 1510 the archbishop of Armagh, Octavian del Palatio, informed Henry VIII that the annual revenues of the Dromore diocese did not exceed £27.6s.8d. Because it was so poor, no one wanted to be bishop there and it had been without one for almost twenty years.[53] It appears that the lands taken over by the Anglo-Normans were not returned to the diocese when their influence declined. "The rectorial tithes and the townland of Kilfeaghan continued to be held under the bishops, until the annexation of the see in 1842."[54] Kilfeaghan is one of eight town lands which make up the area known as Killowen. Seven of them were probably clan lands held by the Magennis clan, but Kilfeaghan was granted as See land to (Protestant) Bishop John Todd in the Iveagh Settlement of 1610.

The pre-Reformation church in Kilbroney parish shows signs of having been built or substantially modified in the fifteenth or sixteenth century.[55] Apart from Magheradrool and Magheralin, nearly all the other pre-Reformation Churches in the diocese were dismantled or replaced in the seventeenth century or after. "The surviving buildings suggest a considerable degree of vitality in the local church on the eve of the Reformation".[56] The Protestant Reformation in Ireland, dated from about 1541 until about 1600. It was much less successful than in England, although it did make significant progress in Ulster. The infusion of religion into the Gaelic social order meant that it was difficult to dislodge, but the rise of the Protestant faith laid the basis for religious division and ultimately political rivalry.

Atkinson has written that in 1534 the Vicar of the Parish was Patrick MacBrun, but it is not clear if he was vicar at the time of the Reformation and whether he or his possible successors opted for the reformed faith or remained with the Catholic Church.[57]

Atkinson records that, "The ancient church continued in possession of the historic Church of Ireland as reformed, but no doubt a large proportion of the population ceased attending its services (even if regularly kept up in those unsettled times) and met for public worship in the woods and hillsides where they were ministered to by priests who adhered to the Roman obedience. One such place of meeting is well known and still at times visited by Roman Catholic devotees, where on the wooded mountain side at the confines of the parish where it adjoins Clonduff there stands a great rock, a portion of whose surface has been levelled and marked with five incised crosses to serve as an altar."[58] The same site was used about 200 years later to celebrate Mass during the penal Days. It is known as *Altnataggart* or the Mass Rock, just across Kilbroney parish boundary in Clonduff, on the Newtown Road.

Fig 4.7 Mass Rock at Altnataggart. The straight line running up the slope on the left the picture marks the boundary between the parish of Kilbroney (left) and the parish of Clonduff (right).

While the three influences of Vikings, Anglo-Normans and the Church had a major impact on Irish society in Medieval times, the social fabric of that society was also changing. The Celtic way of life was being modified by the English authorities, a process which would be speeded up in the following century.

The Native Irish

The Irish had a system of land ownership determined by the clan (family) but the English had a system of personal ownership, whereby land would be inherited by the eldest son on the father's death. In 1541 the Lord Lieutenant introduced a mechanism in which the Irish could surrender their lands and have them returned under the new inheritance system.

The Magennis clan were the most dominant in Iveagh (largely South Down) at this time. However, they were divided into rival groups based in Rathfriland, Corgory (near Jerrettspass), Kilwarlin (near Moira) and Castlewellan. Following the death of Murtagh Magennis of Corgory in 1539, Donal Og Magennis of Rathfriland and Art McPhelim Magennis of Castlewellan both claimed his inheritance. Among those whom the English Lord Lieutenant appointed to arbitrate the dispute was Arthur McGlassney Magennis, holder of the bishop's mensal[59] of Kilbroney.[60]

The outcome of the dispute was that Donal Og retained Rathfriland and Art McPhelim retained Castlewellan. In 1542 they both travelled to London to receive knighthoods. The Magennis clan were conforming to the English system. From 1567 onwards a policy of plantation was introduced in Ulster (which laid the way for the Ulster Plantation in the following century). Under the scheme, a Captain John Sankeye received land in, among other places, "Ballenemoney, Dromrey and Dromseske"[61]. They presumably refer to Ballymoney, Drumreagh and Drumsesk. Twelve years later the order granting the lands was rescinded and the land was returned to the Magennis clan.

If there is direct association between the Magennis clan and four townlands in the Rostrevor area, it appears reasonable to assume that Rostrevor and its surrounding district were within their clan territory. Although there is no direct evidence of a Rory Magennis in Rostrevor in the middle of the 16th Century, one Irish name for Rostrevor is *Caisleán Ruairi* (Rory's Castle). There is no reliable indication of where such a castle was located. The first Ordnance Survey Map (1832) shows what it describes as a "Ruin" on the flat land behind the Ghan filling station. It had disappeared from OS maps by the 1900 edition. This has traditionally been assumed to be the site of Rory's Castle, but there is no physical evidence to support this belief.

In the 16th Century this would probably still have been a marshy area and although the site of the ruins is slightly higher than the surrounding land, it appears an unlikely location for what was presumably a defensive position.

Fig 4.8 Local tradition suggests that Caisleán Ruairi was located in the marshy ground at Point B, because the First Edition of Ordnance Survey maps in 1832 marked that site as having a ruin. A better site for a castle might have been at Point A on the higher ground where the Monument was later built.

There are two places in Rostrevor where a castle might have been built. The first is at the site of the Crag, which is the house at the top of Bridge Street on the right as you face towards the bridge. Because of its elevated position, it can be defended on three sides (the river, the shore and the swamp along the Warrenpoint Road). The other is on the high ground at or immediately behind the Monument, which can also be defended on three sides (the sea on two of them and the swampy ground on the third).

An 1846 tourist guide[62] to the area said of Rostrevor: "Near the centre of the town between the main street and the shore, stood the formerly massive Castle of Rory M'Gennis, a kinsman of the Lord of Iveagh, who formerly owned this region and to whom Rostrevor owes its origin." This presumably refers to the Crag, which probably comes from the Irish *carraig*, meaning a rock or a rock face. This would reflect the steep slope from the river up through Brick Row to the Crag and also the steep slope from the GAA social club car park. Former names for Rostrevor include *Carraig a' bhrachta*, meaning a rock of malting or fermented matter.[63]

However, three years later (1849) in a publication of a more scientific nature, Samuel Lewis wrote of Rostrevor, "This place was anciently called Castle Roe or Rory, from its original founder, Rory, one of the family of the Magennises, lords of Iveagh, of whose baronial castle, subsequently occupied by the Trevor family, there are still some remains near the town."[64] Exactly how near the town is not specified, nor have we any idea in what direction from the town the remains might have been. It conceivably could have been at the Monument, although "near the town" could also refer to the Crag, or even at Point B in Fig. 4.8. So, the two historical references to the castle's remains do little to clarify its original location, especially since another work a century earlier made no mention of any ruins or castle.[65]

There was certainly some form of building at the Monument site. There is no reference to any building or remains in that area on the 1832 first edition Ordnance Survey map, but it clearly shows a ridge of land extending from the Monument northwards, which is at least 50 feet above the surrounding land. That would make it a defensible position.

Fig 4.9 The site behind the Monument

Some understanding of the site can be gained from adopting the principles of hydromorphology[66] to analyse the landforms from the air (Fig 4.10). This shows that the location has been heavily modified by what is called anthropogenic (human) activity. While it may have been a rath at some earlier stage, one interpretation of the site is that it has been modified at a later date, because it has a flattened hilltop, unlike the tops of other hills in the area. It also appears to have a ditch, a defensive wall and a bawn on its outer side. (A bawn is a fortified enclosure around a castle.)

Fig 4.10 Possible interpretation of the site. The photographs for the site are in black and white to make illustration easier.

Viewed from the public area behind the Monument (Fig. 4.11) there also appears to be evidence of a roadway and the remains of a lower enclosure. The site also shows evidence (Fig. 4.12) of what may have been bastions (projecting parts of a fortification built at an angle to the line of a wall, to allow defensive fire in several directions).

The Monument site appears to have been quite extensive. About 150 yards from the Monument, along the ridge towards Drumsesk, are a number of other indications of human modification to the landscape. It is not known is this activity happened at the same time as the development of the site referred to above, or if it happened in a different era.

Fig 4.11 A possible interpretation of the site at ground level. (Photograph taken across the fence from inside the Monument public area.)

Fig 4.12 Possible bastions

Fig 4.13 Aerial photographs of the site showing an approximately rectangular bare patch in the vegetation in (a) (centre right of photograph), (b) (centre) and (c) (bottom left). This is likely to indicate the existence of a building at some previous point.

114

Fig 4.13 (a), (b) and (c) show a rectangular bare patch in one field which may indicate the previous existence of a building there. Fig. 4.13 (d) reveals a number of circular patterns in the vegetation, which suggest either buildings(s) on that site or at least some form of earthworks there. As well as showing modern tractor tyre marks, (d) shows around 10 twin circular markings on the top of the ridge, which are unlikely to have been made by a tractor and indicate some form of circular building or earthworks. No circular markings are found in an adjoining lower field, even though both fields appear to be treated and harvested in a similar manner in recent years. The twin markings are also wider than the obvious vehicle tracks.

While surface vegetation patterns give a rough indication of what might be underneath, a more accurate depiction can be achieved by what is known as sobel edge detection. Fig 4.14 shows a normal aerial photograph of part of the site. It illustrates a brown discolouration in the centre which stands out from the green vegetation.

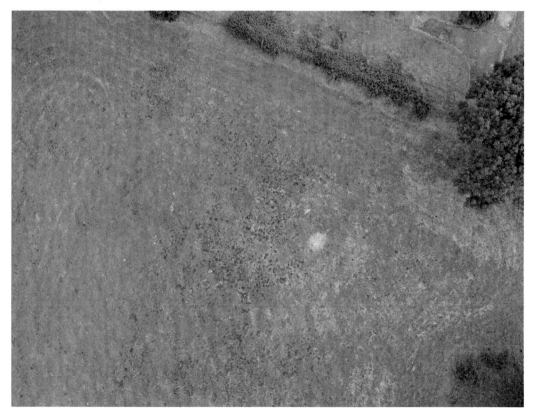

Fig 4.14 Brown discolouration in the centre of the photograph.

Fig 4.15 shows the same photograph analysed by sobel edge detection. It reveals the outline of two rectangular buildings. We do not know what these buildings were or who owned them. However, we have now established that the area immediately behind the Monument has been subject to significant human activity as indicated by landscape analysis. In addition, it is now likely that there were at least two buildings on this site at some point, long before the Monument was erected. Indeed, it might reasonably be assumed that the area which was cleared to build the Monument was part of this site. In recording British imperial history by building a Monument to a British Major-General, its builders may have destroyed more relevant Irish history in the process.[67]

Fig 4.15 showing the outlines of what appears to be two rectangular-shaped buildings close to each other.

While it is highly likely that there was a structure (or structures) of some sort on this site, we do not know if this was the castle of Rory Magennis. It could have been the house built in the early part of the 17th Century by Edward Trevor when, with the backing of the crown, he effectively stole the Magennis lands. For that reason Trevor would be unlikely to want the Magennis Castle to be recorded in contemporary maps at the time. He might even have adapted the castle in his own interests on the same site, or possibly demolished it and built a large house.

We know that the Trevor family had a house somewhere in Rostrevor. Assuming that the Trevors were still living in that same house in 1662, a friend of the family[68] who was visiting Rostrevor with the newly married Mark Trevor, described the house as "indifferent and that's all, for it is but very ordinary for a person of his quality and he deserves better"[69] Whether that very ordinary house was located behind the Monument is unclear, but the basic evidence at the moment suggests that there was one and possibly two buildings on the site and the remains of defensive fortifications.

We might reasonably assume that the sketch map (Fig 4.16) offers the best interpretation of the information which we have available. It suggests that this is a complex site which would require detailed archaeological investigation to finally reveal what was actually there. However, the site is on private property and should not be interfered with in any way. Further investigations should be left to the proper authorities. The site can be viewed from the Rostrevor-Warrenpoint road and from the back of the Monument public area, as was done in this study.

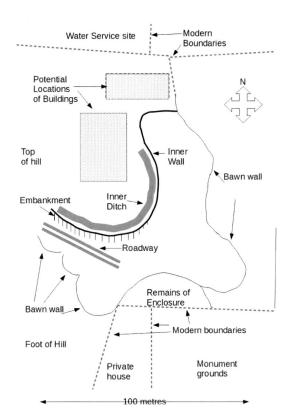

Fig. 4.16 Site map showing possible location of buildings on the site. The Monument is where the words "Monument grounds" are.

So as the Medieval period ran its course, the old Celtic system was being replaced by a new social, economic and political order which was slowly taking hold in the second half of the 16th Century. The influence of the Vikings had largely waned, and the remaining impact of the Anglo-Normans was largely in administration.

Only the influence of the Catholic Church survived, but it now had competition from the Protestant faith, following the Reformation. Although the Magennis clan would survive for another 150 years, its power and influence were on the decline. The last remnant of the Magennis clan is a memorial stone reported in 1901 to lie close to the East wall of the old church of Clonduff. Previously "broken into pieces and one small portion lost"[70], it was later fully restored.

Despite their attempts to adapt to English ways and their professed loyalty to the crown, the Magennis clan soon found themselves outwitted and gradually landless by a new ruling elite in Ireland. Rostrevor, in the heart of Magennis country, was about to witness a new invasion in what was to prove the most significant in its modern history. The process of Anglicising Rostrevor on a large scale was about to begin. A new chapter was opening up on its history and that chapter will form the first section of the second part of Rostrevor's history, place and people.

Chapter Endnotes

1   Todd J H (ed) (1867) *Cogadh Gaedhel re Gallaibh* (The War of the Gael with the Gall) Original Irish Text translated by J H Todd London. Original probably written between 1103 and 1111, p 7.

2   Todd p 7

3   It may have been called Cuan Snámh Aigneach (the harbour of the fast-flowing sea channel) before then. See: Murray L (1914) Omeath *Journal of the County Louth Archaeological Society*, Vol 3 No 3, pp 213-231.

4   The 'hag' may refer to the outline of the rocks which shape the local mountain.

5   Author Unknown (Late 15th Century) Annals of Ulster The Annals of Ulster Corpus of Electronic Texts Edition: T1100001A. University College Cork 2020 p 289.

6   Neill K (1991) One Fair County.... *Archaeology Ireland* Vol 5 No 2, p 10.

7   *Annals of Ulster* p 295.

8   *Annals of Ulster* p 299.

9   Clinton M (2013) The Monastery of Linn Duchaill *Journal of the County Louth Archaeological and Historical Society* Vol. 28, No. 1 (2013), pp. 22-38.

10   'Lost' early Viking site in Co Louth one of 'most important' in world, Irish Times, 10 October 2011.

11   Downham C (2010) Viking Camps in Ninth-century Ireland: Sources, Location and Interactions. *Academia* pp 5-6.

12   *Annals of Ulster* p 285.

13   *Annals of Ulster* p 311.

14   Woulfe P (1923) *Sloinnte Gaedheal* is Gall Irish Names and Surnames. M H Gill & Son Dublin p 387.

15   Woulfe p 511.

16   Bardon J (2001) A History of Ulster Blackstaff Press, p 32.

17   Russell C W, Pendergast J P (eds) (1872) *Calendar of the State Papers relating to Ireland of the Reign of James I 1608-1610* Preserved in HM Public Record Office and Elsewhere, p xi.

18   Wright T (1894) *The Historical Works of Gerald's Cambrensis* (first published 1187) Internet Archive p 277

19   Lawlor H C (1938) The Identification of the Castle of Magh Cobha *Ulster Journal of Archaeology* Vol 1, 1938 p 84.

20   Mooney B J (1950) *Place-Names of Rostrevor* p 7.

21   *Annals of Ulster* p 193.

22   *Annals of Ulster* p 1212.

23   *Annals of Four Masters* (compiled 1632-36, author unknown) Corpus of Electronic Texts, University College Cork, 2020 pp 1211-1213.

24   See curious ireland.ie

25   *Annals of Ulster* pp 1211-1213.

26   *Annals of Ulster* pp 1211-1213.

27   McNeill T E (1980). *Anglo-Norman Ulster*, Institute of Irish Studies, Queen's University, Belfast, p 23.

28   Ministry of Finance (1966) *An Archaeological Survey of County Down* HMSO p 213.

29   Waterman D M, Collins A E P, Morton W R M, Jope M (1952) Excavations at Greencastle, Co Down 1951, *Ulster Journal of Archaeology* Vol 15 pp87-102.

30   Ministry of Finance, p 103.

31   Corrway L (2015) The History and Architecture of King John's Castle in Carlingford: A View on the West Side, *Journal of the County Louth Archaeological and Historical Society*, Vol 28, No 3 pp 351-360. De Lacy was the son of Hugh de Lacy I who died in1186, "when his head was cut off by an Irishman he was showing how to use a pick" p 351.

32   Corrway p 352.

33   Baronies (headed by a baron) were sub-divisions of a county, usually named after places which had been important to the native Irish before the Anglo-Normans came. They were sometimes referred to as kingdoms, hence The Kingdom of Mourne.

34   Iveagh *(Uíbh Eachach)* means 'descendants of Echu' which was originally part of the kingdom of Ulaid.

35   *Archaeological Survey of County Down* p 105.

36   See: McCotter P (2019) The Origins of the Parish in Ireland Proceedings of the Royal Irish Academy: Archaeology, Culture, History, Literature, RIA Volume 119C, 2019 pp. 37-6.

37   See: Sinéad Ní Ghabhláin (1996) The Origin of Medieval Parishes in Gaelic Ireland: The Evidence from Kilfenora, *The Journal of the Royal Society of Antiquaries of Ireland* Vol. 126 (1996), pp. 37-61.

38   Atkinson E D (1829) *Dromore: An Ulster Diocese* p 70 (digitised by University College Cork).

39   In Medieval times a mark was worth two thirds of a pound (about 66 pence). It was not represented by a coin but was used mainly for accountancy purposes.

40   Lawlor H J (1911) A Calendar of the Register of Archbishop Sweteman, Proceedings of the Royal Irish Academy Vol 29, Section C p 281.

41   Mooney p 7.

42   Reeves W (1847) *Ecclesiastical Antiquities of Down, Connor and Dromore, Consisting of A Taxation of Those Dioceses*, Dublin p 115.

43   Atkinson p 309.

44   Reeves p 115.

45   Agholy was a common first name among the Magennis clann, as in the townland name, Ballyagholy, meaning Agholy's homestead.

46   Jefferies H A (1997) The Diocese of Dromore on the Eve of the Tudor Reformation, Chapter 6 in Proudfoot L (ed) *Down, History and Society*, Geography Publications, p 124.

47   The Irish Medieval Office of erenagh (Irish airchinnech) was responsible for receiving parish revenue in the form of tithes and rents. It means "son of the Lord of the Church". It has given rise to the modern surname MacEnerney. They were initially the head or superior of a monastic settlement and although they had received minor Holy Orders, they did not all necessarily become clerics. Their estates were transferred to the bishops in the twelfth and early thirteenth century and they became the chief tenants of episcopal lands. They were generally able to speak Latin into the early 17th Century at least. See: Jeffries H A (1999) Erenaghs in Pre-Plantation Ulster: An Early Seventeenth-Century Account. *Archivium Hibernicum* Vol 53 pp 16-19.

48   Jeffries p 127.

49   Jeffries p 129. The surname McEntegart means "Son of the priest" (Mac an tSagairt) and MacAnespie means "Son of the Bishop" (Mac an Easpaig).

50   Gwynn A (1946) *The medieval province of Armagh 1470-1546* W Tempest Dun Dealgan Press, pp 141-9.

51   Oddly, in 2019 it returned to that same arrangement following the resignation of Bishop John McAreavey.

52   Reeves W p 103.

53   Jeffries p 131.

54   Reeves, p 309.

55   Ministry of Finance pp 303, 307-8.

56   Jeffries p 129.

57   Atkinson p 70.

58   Atkinson, p 70.

59   Mensal means money set aside for the maintenance of a priest or bishop.

60   O'Sullivan H (1997) The Magennis Lordship of Iveagh in the Early Modern Period, 1534 to 1691 in Proudfoot L (ed) *Down History ad Society* Geography Publications, p 160.

61   O'Sullivan p 162.

62   *A Picturesque Handbook to Carlingford Bay and the Watering Places in its Vicinity* (1846) No author. Published by Greer and dedicated to His Royal Highness Prince Albert, Patron Carlingford Lough Regatta, p 37.

63   Mooney p 12.

64   *Lewis S (1849) Topographical Dictionary of Ireland* 2nd edition Vol 2, p 539.

65   Harris W (1744) *The Antient and Present State of the County Down* Dublin p 87.

66   Hydromorphology analyses the landscape to determine how human and physical activity has influenced rivers and their environment.

67   Noted Rostrevor historian, the late Robert Linden, told me of nearby buildings which were built from dressed stone, probably from a ruined castle or large house. The next volume of this history will look at this subject in more detail.

68   The friend was Katherine Philips (1631-1664), also known as the "Matchless Orinda". She was the author of the first English-language play written by a woman and performed on the professional stage and she may also have been the first published lesbian poet in the English language.

69   O'Sullivan H (1985) *The Trevors of Rosetrevor, A British Colonial Family in 17th Century Ireland* Unpublished M Litt Thesis TCD p 187. She also referred to "the most barren parts of it that are hilly and near the sea but that there is very little wood and the prospect not in the least pleasant", which suggests that the oak wood near the Quay is not an ancient Irish oak wood, but a more recent planation.

70   Author un-named (1901) The Magennis Armorial Stone (1901). *Ulster Journal of Archaeology*, Vol 7 No 1, p 63.

ROSTREVOR PLACE-NAMES

Rostrevor village.

The Drumreagh and Knockbarragh Valley

Townland Names

The history of Rostrevor cannot be fully appreciated without an understanding of its geography and the place-names used to describe it. The local place-names were originally in Irish, most of which survive today in townland names. A townland is an ancient Irish division of land, usually anywhere from 100 to 500 acres. Its boundaries are normally marked by a water course ranging in scale from a seugh to a river, although other physical features are also sometimes used.

Irish townlands were later adopted by the Anglo-Normans and the English as administrative divisions and their boundaries were then used to delineate parishes and ultimately counties. County boundaries are therefore generally based on townlands, which means that the border's irregular passage across the Irish landscape reflects a series of townland boundaries.

The boundary between the parishes of Kilbroney and Clonduff is marked by townland boundaries (in red) which are based on two head-streams of the Drumreagh (Ghann) River.

Many townlands were sub-divided into Upper and Lower divisions by the British authorities in the 19th Century for administrative purposes, including taxation and population census. Despite that, most townlands have retained their original names in Irish, although they have been generally Anglicised to various degrees in spelling and pronunciation. So not only do townland names offer a framework for geographical location, they also provide an understanding of the landscape and/or the history of that area.

Townlands were previously used for postal addresses, but two factors have changed this: the local council's introduction of road names (many of them inappropriate and sometimes inaccurate) and the application of post codes, which means addresses require just a house number and street name. As a result, townlands are now used only for administrative and legal purposes.

Thus local knowledge of townland locations and their names has declined significantly in recent years. Older people still proudly refer to their native townland as a badge of identity and origin, as indicated by the inclusion of townland names on many headstones in local cemeteries. To preserve that tradition, the townlands of the Rostrevor area are listed here with a map to show their location.

The difficulty in determining the meaning of townland names lies in trying to decipher which Irish word(s) the current Anglicised version comes from. That depends to a large extent on penetrating the local accent and pronunciation, which means that there is sometimes more than one possible explanation proposed for a townland name.

The translations used here are based largely on two sources: Rev Bernard Mooney's *Place Names of Rostrevor* (1950) and *Place-Names of Northern Ireland, Volume 1 County Down, Newry and South-West Down* (1992) by Gregory Toner and Mícheál Ó Mainnín. In addition, I have added some locally-based information which may offer clarification in some instances.

Superimposed on our townland names in Irish are more recent place names in English, which have been used to varying degrees by Rostrevor people for the past century or two. They tend to be based on the names of local people or some particular physical feature or activity. They are still widely used by local inhabitants and they are employed in this book on the basis that any description of Rostrevor's history, place and people should be written in the language of its people.

There are many other original Irish names and more recent English names which apply to specific places within the Rostrevor area. They will require more research to verify in terms of derivation and location and they will be included in the next volume.

Townland boundaries are marked by thin white lines. The parish boundary is marked by a wider white line. This map based on the 50K Townlands data set released under Open Government Licence. Townland names are taken from Ordnance Survey Edition 1 (1832 - 1846).

1 Ballyagholy	13 Ballyneddan	25 Levallyreagh
2 Ballincurry	14 Ballyneddan Upper	26 Moygannon
3 Ballincurry Upper	15 Drumreagh	27 Newtown
4 Ballindoalty	16 Drumreagh Upper	28 Newtown Upper
5 Ballindoalty Upper	17 Drumsesk	29 Rostrevor
6 Ballinran	18 Kilbroney	30 Rostrevor Upper
7 Ballinran Upper	19 Kilbroney Upper	31 Rostrevor Mountains
8 Ballintur	20 Kilfeaghan	32 Tamnyveagh
9 Ballintur Upper	21 Kilfeaghan Upper	33 The Point Park
10 Ballyedmond	22 Killowen Mountains	
11 Ballyedmond Upper	23 Knockbarragh	
12 Ballymoney	24 Levallyclanone	

Meanings of Townland Names

Ballincurry: *Baile an Chorraigh*, the place/homestead/townland of the marsh/bog.

Ballindoalty: *Baile an Dhubhaltaigh*, Dubhaltach's place/home/townland.

Ballinran: *Baile an Reann*, The place/townland of the point (presumably referring to Killowen Point).

Ballintur: *Baile an Toir*, The townland/place of the bush/shrub/clump/tuft.

Ballyagholy: *Baile Eachmhílidh*, Agholy's home/homestead/place. (Agholy was a common name among the Magennis clan in South Down.)

Ballyedmond: *Baile Éamainn*, Edmond's place/home/townland.

Ballyneddan: *Baile an Fheadáin*, The townland/place of the stream.

Drumsesk: *Droim Seasc* The barren ridge or hill.

Kilbroney: *Cill Brónaigh*, Church of Bronagh, the townland which gave its name to the parish.

Kilfeaghan: *Cill Féichín*, (Saint) Féichín's Church. Toner and Ó Mainnín query this explanation, saying there is nothing to connect St Féichín (who founded a monastery at Termonfechin) with the Diocese of Dromore. However, geography shows that Kilfeaghan can be seen from Termonfechin. (See Chapter 3.)

Kilfeaghan at the Eastern edge of both Kilbroney Parish and the Diocese of Dromore, with Knockshee on the left. Formal Mountain on the right is in the Diocese of Down and Connor.

Killowen: *Cill Abhainn* Church of the river. Killowen is included here even though it is not a townland. Traditionally it included the seven townlands of Ballinran, Ballyneddan, Ballyedmond, Ballincurry, Ballindoalty, Ballintur and Tamnyveagh, although many of these have since been divided into Upper and Lower divisions.

Traditionally translated as Eoin's or John's Church, Chapter 3 here suggests that local dialect indicates it is more likely to mean church of the river.

Killowen Point at high tide.

Knockbarragh: *Cnoc Bearach*, Hill of heifers.

Levallyclanone: *Leathbhaile Chlann Eoghain*. Half townland of Eoghan's family/descendants. It is possible that "clan" in the English form may be *cluain* (a meadow) rather than *clann* (extended family). However, the hilly nature of the townland may rule this out. Although the "family/descendants" is the generally agreed explanation of the name, it is not clear why it should be a half townland. It certainly has been artificially created because two of its boundaries are perfectly straight lines, which suggests that it was probably a portion of land taken from the original townland of Kilbroney.

This photograph shows a long field boundary marked by both trees and a wall running in a straight line from the Kilbroney Road (at the bottom) up to Big Dan's Wood.

The red line shows the straight townland boundary between Levallyclanone (left) and Kilbroney (right) as marked by modern field boundaries. The townland boundary would have been there first, although it is not clear how it would have been marked.

Levallyreagh: *Leathbhaile Riabhach*, Grey half-townland. Another half townland, but this time there are no straight lines in its boundaries.

Moygannon: *Maigh Ó gCanann*, O'Cannon's plain.

Newtown: This is one of the few townland names in English. It appears to date from the end of the 18th Century. The building of Newtown Road began in 1816.

The Point Park: Another modern English name. It presumably refers to the area from which Killowen Point can be viewed.

Rostrevor: perhaps the most disputed of all the townland names. Its original Irish name(s) was later replaced or adapted by foreign landlords as a form of self-promotion. Earlier names for Rostrevor include *Cairrge Breaca* (speckled rocks) and *Carraig brachain* (rocks of fermented matter), either of which presumably gave rise to the English form, Carrickavraghad.   More traditionally in the area, Rostrevor is known in Irish as *Caisleán Ruairi*, meaning Ruairi's Castle. The local Gaelic football club uses this name. It refers to the castle of Ruairi Magennis (see Chapter 4).

There is a local tradition that Rostrevor's original name is the Irish *Ros Trá Mór* (or possibly *Ros Trá Mhór*, depending on grammar and local pronunciation in Medieval Ireland) meaning the wood (or wooded headland) at the big strand. The name does not appear in any written records, but the language of the people often differed from the language of those in authority. Most of the names used by Rostrevor people in the past two centuries (as listed in the following pages) do not appear on any official documents. It is also possible that *Caisleán Ruairi* was in or at the *Ros Trá Mór*. This latter name may have been Anglicised to "Rostrevor" by the Welsh landlord, Edward Trevor, who found the pronunciation similar to his wife's name, Rose Trevor. ("Rose" may have been pronounced "Ros" in the 17th Century.)

An alternative explanation is that since *rhos* in Welsh means a moorland or even a coastal slope, did Trevor simply give the place a name which staked his claim to ownership of the area: Trevor's moorland/coastal slope? The name was later further adapted to Rosstrevor by the Ross landlords. Adapting (or even adopting) a placename to suit a surname has been a common theme in the history of Irish landlordism, in an attempt to claim legitimacy to dubious ownership. Even today those appointed to the House of Lords use a geographical location in their title. The local council currently utilises the form, *Ros Treabhair*, Trevor's Wood to indicate the townland as a footnote on its street names. This is a combination of the Irish word *Ros*, meaning a wood and the English surname Trevor, after Edward Trevor who replaced the Magennis clan as one of the main landowners in South Down. From a wide range of options, it is perhaps the least appropriate. On the basis of local practice, *Caisleán Ruairi* would appear to be the most reliable form.

Ros Trá Mór/Mhór? (The wood or wooded headland at the big strand.)

Tamnyveagh: *Tamhnaigh Bheithe*, The fine field of the birch.

Mountain names: the names of local mountains are interchangeable between Irish and English. So *Leacan Beag* is referred to as "Wee Leacan" (occasionally "Wee Loughan") and *Leacan Mór* as "Big Leacan". Indeed the pronunciation can differ on opposite sies of Leacan Mór, between the Kilbroney Valley and the Drumreagh valley. Similarly, the English "Cloughmore" is also referred to as *Cloch Mór*. The word Slieve (Irish: *sliabh*) means "mountain". In local speech it is sometimes shortened to "Slive" as in "Slive Roe" (*Sliabh Rua*) or "Sleh Ban" (*Sliabh Bán*). Occasionally names are given an extra syllable as in Sliver-oe (*Sliabh Rua*).

Other names of interest:

Ballynagelty: *Baile na geilte*, The place of the crazed woman. This refers to a woman who supposedly saw her two sons drown in Carlingford Lough while out fishing and she went insane as a result. It refers mainly to the top of the hill, near where there is now a seat. It also applies to the slope below it, which has more recently been rather insultingly referred to as Kodak Corner by those who show no appreciation of, or respect for, Rostrevor's history or culture. By placing the wooden nameplate *An Radharc* (meaning The View) at that spot, Sean Tinnelly offered a more appropriate alternative.

Ballynagelty overlooking Carlingford Lough

Covernnestrade: *Cuibhreann na straide*, the allotment of the street, previously called *Leathbhaile sraide* meaning the half townland of the street. Covernnestrade in my lifetime referred to the land immediately across Kilbroney Road from the gate into the old cemetery, to the right of what is now the upper entrance into Mourne Wood. In Kilbroney it was known as glebe land, meaning that it was church land which a clergyman could use for income in return for pastoral duties. It adjoins Levallyclanone, another half townland.

Covernnestrade is the area across the road behind and to the right of the road nameplate as seen from inside the old cemetery. It was presumably part of the original monastic settlement which includes the church ruins.

Names Used by Rostrevor People

It is both respectful and appropriate that any description of Rostrevor's history, place and people should be written in the language used by Rostrevor people for generations. So, the locations referred to in this book are identified here, in alphabetical order, in what might be termed the language of Rostrevor. Not all of the names here are used in this Part I of this history. Those which are not mentioned will appear in a future volume. Others will be added later.

Bandy Bridge: the bridge on the Kilbroney Road just on the Hilltown side of the cemetery.

Benvenue: the viewpoint which is now the highest part of Cherry Hill. It is also the name of the house at the bottom of the Dunn's Hill, behind the wall at the head of the Doctor's Loanin.

Biddy Doyle's Corner: where the Lower Knockbarragh Road meets Coyle's Hill and the Yellow Road. Biddy Doyle (no relation to the Doyles who live there now) lived in a house straight across from the Lower Knockbarragh Road. There is no trace of it now.

Big Dan's Wood: now referred to by the Ordnance Survey as Ballymoney Wood.

Campbell's Jetty: the upright remains of a wooden jetty about 200 yards on the Kilkeel side of the current jetty at the back of the Dock.

The last surviving uprights of Campbell's jetty.

Crab Island: the pile of stones on a rock outcrop offshore at the Monument corner.

Crotlieve (pronounced "Crotley", as in "Up at Crotley"): the area immediately to the South of Crotlieve Mountain (from the Irish *Croit-shliabh*, meaning "hump mountain").

Crotlieve Loanin (as in "across Crotley Loanin"): The loanin from Kilbroney Road to Newtown Road, at the base of Crotlieve Mountain.

Fallagh (possibly Fallow): the flatish area beginning where the top forest road parallel to Newtown Road levels off. There used to be a wooden gate there which was called Fallagh Gate. Forestry workers had to be there by 8 am to start work.

Fr Matthew Hall (also known as the Temperance Hall): the old hall at the back of the houses in Water Street (on your left as you walk down) which was briefly mis-named Harmony Hill in the 1960s.

It is named after Fr Theobald Matthew (1790-1856) who founded the Catholic Total Abstinence Society, forerunner of the Pioneer Total Abstinence Association. There is a statue to him in Cork city.

Gray's Back: the narrow roadway running from the Warrenpoint Road to the footbridge over the Moygannon River, past Warrenpoint GAA pitch.

Horner's Loanin: now called Horner's Lane.

Kate's Strame (Stream): the stream crossing under Newtown Road about half a mile down from Crotlieve Loanin.

Kilbroney: this word has two applications: (a) the townland on the Western side of the Kilbroney Valley which runs roughly North from Rostrevor and (b) the Catholic and Church of Ireland parish in which Rostrevor is situated. Neither has any

Fr Matthew Hall

connection to the mis-named Kilbroney Park, often shortened to Kilbroney, which now misrepresents the original use and meaning of the word.

Kilbroney Park: the four houses on the Kilbroney Road about a mile and a half from Rostrevor.

Kilbroney River: the river which runs from Shanlieve to the sea through the Fairy Glen in its lower course. Its upper stage is normally referred to as the Yellow Water, presumably because of the discolouration caused by the high level of peat sediment in the water.

Lennon's Corner: the junction between the Greenpark Road and the Levallyreagh Road.

Martin's Low Gates/Martin's Top Gates: the two entrances into what is now rather oddly called Mourne Wood. Both entrances were later called Cornwall's Low and Top Gates for a time.

Moygannon Bridge: the bridge at Moygannon River on the Road to Warrenpoint. The river marks the edge of the parish of Kilbroney.

Peadar's Hill (pronounced Pether's Hill): the steepest hill on the Drumreagh Road about two miles from Rostrevor.

Pothill: *a clachan* (see The Close in the following pages) on a river terrace (see Chapter 1) overlooking Drumreagh River, which was probably a crossing point before the new bridge was built.

Reed Hall: the area at the summit of the Kilbroney Road on the way to Hilltown. The hill on both the Hilltown and Rostrevor sides is referred to as Reed Hall Hill.

Reed Hall Hill from the Hilltown side in the 1940s

Ross's Wood: the wooded area behind the Castle and extending to the high ground above Cherry Hill.

Spallick: the area on Leacan Mór near the Bucht.

The Back of the Dock (but never referred to as the Back of the Quay): the area immediately on the Kilkeel side of the Dock where there is now an extended slipway and a new jetty, constructed in 2008. They can be credited to Gerry Sloan and his team.

The Back Road: now called Cloughmore Road.

The Barrack Green (as in "Up the Barrack Green"): the area in front of and leading up to the sheltered dwelling complex behind the Church of Ireland. The original building where the complex now stands was a British army barracks.

What's left of The Barrack Green.

The Black Loanin: the track running off to the left from lower Newtown Road just before the bridge over the Kilbroney River.

The Bucht: the circular walled enclosure on Leacan Mór near Big Dan's Wood, which was used as a place for herding sheep. The word appears to come from Lowland Scots (an English language dialect), meaning a sheepfold, especially one in which ewes were kept at milking time.

The Bog (as in "up at the Bog"): the area between the Lower Knockbarragh Road and the Drumreagh Road. It extends towards the Mullaghgariff Road (*mullach garbh*: rough or rugged high point), colloquially known as "The Molly". It has now largely been reclaimed into fertile farmland.

The Burma Road: the forest road, beyond Fiddler's Green, running parallel to the Kilkeel Road. It was given its name by the forestry workers who built it during the Second World War, when news bulletins carried information about the road the Japanese were building in Burma. A house known as the Classha or Shepherd's Cottage in that area was demolished and the rubble was used as fill for part of the road. (This was told to me by the late Barney Smyth, who worked in The Wood.)

The Castle (also known as the Nuns' Castle): the large house, formerly a residence of the Ross's, on the Greenpark Road. It was later occupied by the Missionary Sisters of Our Lady of the Apostles, hence its alternative name.

The Chapel Hill: the hill from the village to the chapel, now called Church Street - a street which previously ended at the bottom of the hill.

The Close: formerly a group of houses on the low side of Kilbroney Road near Crotlieve Loanin. In Irish it is referred to as a *clachan*, meaning a number of houses in close proximity.

The Convent: the building fronting the road beside the chapel. It was part of the original Convent of Mercy School.

The Corner of the Town: the name used by those from Ballymoney, Drumreagh, Knockbarragh and Levallyreagh for the point where the Greenpark Road meets Mary Street. The houses on the left (as you face up The Greenpark Road) were previously called Glen Alpine. The new houses on that site are called Kilbroney Court.

The Crabapple Turn: the corner in the road near the top entrance to what is now called St Bronagh's Primary School. It takes its name from the crabapple trees which grew there.

The Dock, also known as the Quay: the pier across the road from Campbell's garage.

The Doctor's Loanin: now renamed Forestbrook Avenue. Where it meets the Kilbroney Road is referred to as the Head of the Doctor's Loanin.

The Duke's Corner (pronounced Dukesis): the first corner on the Kilbroney Road up past the graveyard. It is named because Jack and Lizzy the Duke (proper name McGivern) lived there.

The Dunn's Hill (previously known as Dan Dunn's Hill): the next hill up past the chapel on the Kilbroney Road, which is believed to have been near the home place of 1798 United Irishman, Thomas Dunn.

The Eel Hole: the land on the left as you travel along the top of Reed Hall going to Hilltown. Formerly a bog, it was originally used as a water supply for the lower Kilbroney Road and part of Rostrevor. The water was passed through two settlement tanks and filtrated in what was known as the Waterworks (since demolished) at the point on the Kilbroney Road marking one Irish mile from Rostrevor Square. Those living up the road past the Waterworks did not have access to piped water because it was untreated. The Eel Hole has now largely been drained and reclaimed.

The Eel Hole, looking towards Rostrevor.

The Ghann River: also known as Drumreagh River. The name comes from the Irish *ganntanas* meaning a scarcity - the river often has a greatly reduced flow in the summer.

The Ghann Stream: the stream which drains from that marshy area behind the petrol station on the Warrenpoint Road and flows under the road. Its name has the same origin as that of the Ghann River.

The Glen Stream: the stream which rises above the car park just below Cloughmore and flows to join the Kilbroney River. It is the first stream you cross on your way up the Fairy Glen. Its name was first recorded in writing on the Ordnance Survey Third Edition Maps (1900-1907).

The Green Road: on your way down on the tarred road from the carpark below Cloughmore, take the road to the right at the sharp hairpin bend. It runs from there to join the top forest road which goes up to Fallagh.

The Gwynne's Loanin: From the junction of the Upper and Lower Knockbarragh Roads down as far as the right-angled bend in the road.

The Gwynne's Loanin

The Hall Bridge: the bridge over Drumreagh River on the Warrenpoint Road.

The Lane (also known as the Back Lane): now called Water Street.

The Lodge: the house which originally stood in the Meadow on the high ground where there is now an un-tarred car park facing Killowen Terrace.

The Lodge

The Meadow: Now re-named by the local council as Kilbroney Park, even though it has no connection with Kilbroney.

The Mill: Forestbrook Mill.

The Monument: now referred to as the Ross Monument on the Warrenpoint Road.

The Park

The Park: the townland of Levallyclanone.

The Park Loanin: now (rather politely) called Park Lane. It is the laneway through Levallyclanone.

The Pleasure Ground: the area of trees and bushes on both sides of, and at the back of, the Lodge in the Meadow.

The Post Office Hill (previously called Emmerson's Hill): Mary Street.

The Promenade: the grassy area along the shore across the road from Victoria Square, which the council in its ignorance now calls Rostrevor Foreshore Amenity Area.

The Promenade: the grassy area between the Shore Road and Carlingford Lough, just this side of where the Kilbroney River enters the sea. The Ghann (Drumreagh) River can also be seen entering the sea (top left).

The Quarter Hill: the hill on the way up the Upper Knockbarragh Road.

The Reservoir: the circular dam to the right of the roadway up to the forest car park. It previously supplied Rostrevor's water system.

The Salmon Leap: the small waterfall on the Kilbroney River as it flows through the Fairy Glen.

The Salmon Leap in full flood.

The Scholars' Pad: the pathway across the mountain from the top of Kilbroney to Drumreagh, which was used by Kilbroney children on their way to Drumreagh School.

The Sliding Rock: the steeply-sloped rock on the mountain side of Drumreagh Road just below what was Drumreagh School.

The Slope: The shore area across the road from the Turn of the Quay.

The Tide: (as in, "Were you in the tide today?"): other people call it the sea.

Limerick's Colin Ryan in the 2023 Poc Fada na hÉireann in the Cooley Mountains with (moving from the bottom up the picture), the Omeath shoreline, "The Tide", Rostrevor and the high Mournes in the background.

The Turn of the Quay: where the Cloughmore Road (more accurately known as the Back Road) meets the Shore Road.

The Valley: the colloquial name for the Valley Dye Works, where cloth was dyed. The site is now occupied by Kilbroney Homes. The Dye Works was connected across the Kilbroney River by a rough wooden footbridge (referred to as "the plank") which allowed access for those workers who lived in Kilbroney. The Valley and the Wood were reliable sources of employment for many years.

The Waste Land: the area beyond the Bog at the top of Lower Knockbarragh Road. It has now largely been reclaimed.

The Wood (as in "He works in the Wood"): the Forestry Service's coniferous forest, first planted in the 1930s.

What used to be the waste land.

The Author

Professor Patrick Murphy is a native of Rostrevor where he still lives. He is a former Director and Chief Executive of Belfast Institute of Further and Higher Education. In recent years he has sat, and continues to sit, on the boards of various public bodies here and in England across a wide range of disciplines including education at every level from nursery to university, heritage, medical research ethics, agriculture, agri-food and biosciences, local government, pharmacy and environment. He has contributed to many newspapers and journals and he currently writes a weekly column for the Irish News. He has displayed a lifelong commitment to preserving the character of Rostrevor, its people and its culture.